HELLO, JELL-O!

VICTORIA BELANGER

with Raquel D'Apice

Photography by Angie Cao

HELLO, JELL-O!

50+ inventive recipes for gelatin treats and jiggly sweets

TEN SPEED PRESS

BERKELEY

CONTENTS

ACKNOWLEDGMENTS ~ vi

INTRODUCTION ~ 1

CHAPTER 1

TIPS, TRICKS, TOOLS, AND TECHNIQUES ~ 7

CHAPTER 2

SUSPENDED FRUIT AND MORE! ~ 17

pomegranate berry salad ~ cheery cherry salad ~ million dollar gelatin ~ carrot cake ~ nut 'n' honey ~ orange spice

CHAPTER 3

CREAMY AND DREAMY ~29

green milk tea ~ lemon poppy seed ~ key lime pie ~ creamsicle ~ chocolate raspberry mousse cups ~ apricot cream ~ crème brûlée ~ chai tea panna cotta ~ grasshopper pie

CHAPTER 4

BOOZY MOLDS ~ 45

mimosa ~ white sangria ~ sparkling champagne and strawberries ~ mojito ~ piña colada ~ pear and lychee martini ~ raspberry cosmo ~ coffee kahlúa ~ mudslide

CHAPTER 5
FRUIT-AND-CREAM LAYERED MOLDS ~ 59

peaches and cream ~ blueberry yogurt ~ cherry cream ~ orange chocolate ~ minty watermelon ice cream ~ classic rainbow mold ~ banana cream pie

CHAPTER 6
SEASONAL HOLIDAY MOLDS ~ 77

berry fourth of july ~ brains!!! ~ pumpkin pie ~ eggnog rum ~ hot chile chocolate ~ gingerbread men ~ spiced wassail

CHAPTER 7
AMERICANA AND OTHER FAVORITES ~ 87

petite watermelons ~ tiramisu ~ samoa ~ root beer float squares ~ new york cheesecake ~ chocolate peanut butter cups ~ peanut butter and jelly ~ strawberry nutella ~ marshmallow butterscotch

CHAPTER 8
VEGAN DELIGHTS ~ 105

coconut raspberry agar ~ watermelon basil agar ~ rhubarb rosemary agar ~ maple soy agar ~ vanilla clementine panna cotta

ABOUT THE AUTHOR ~ 116

MEASUREMENT CONVERSION CHARTS ~ 117

INDEX ~ 118

ACKNOWLEDGMENTS

Thank you to all the great folks who worked on the book, including the fantastically funny and witty comedic writer Raquel D'Apice, recipe tester Bora Chang, photographer Angie Cao and her assistant Calvin Ma and intern Jenn Bakos, food stylist Kim Kissling and her assistants Jason Wheeler and Jody Kicherer, prop stylist Emma Star Jensen, designer Betsy Stromberg, agent Pilar Queen at McCormick & Williams, and editor Lisa Westmoreland at Ten Speed Press.

And special thanks to my mother, father, and all my friends and family who encouraged my gelatinous creativity, scoured the thrift stores of America for vintage molds, showered me with recipe suggestions, and tirelessly taste-tested all my molded creations.

Without all of you, this book would not have been possible.

Thank you!

Victoria Belanger

INTRODUCTION

JELL-O HAS A BAD RAP. Once a playful staple at the pool parties of our child-hoods, it has since been consigned to the categories of "things you feed to people in hospitals," "items in Chinese buffets," and "ways we didn't want to remember Bill Cosby." Some of us harbor vague memories of Jell-O recipes from the 1950s—instructions calling for fruity gelatin and mincemeat; recipes that layer lemon-flavored gelatin with olives, green peppers, carrots, and canned pineapple juice. But these are memories we try very hard to suppress. As adults, we look at Jell-O in a practical way: "It is a good food," we say to ourselves, "for people aged seven and under or ninety-one and above. It's perfect for people with nominally functional teeth who are in bed before eight thirty in the evening."

It's not that we don't have wonderful memories of Jell-O, because we do. But we are adults now, right? We sit back and eat the things people consider *adult* desserts, like gelato, lavender macaroons, and biscotti (whose crumbs invariably wind up in my hair, no matter how carefully I attempt to eat them). We make reservations at the kinds of restaurants where even the *word* Jell-O is not allowed—places where the wines are described as "warm and floral, with a hint of earth" and where it's not okay to just pour ketchup on everything. We are adults who buy the Wednesday print edition of the *New York Times* in order to read the Dining section and who scroll through foodie blogs, trying to perfect our homemade butternut squash ravioli and cucumber-mint martinis. Asking us if we still eat Jell-O is like asking us what percentage of our week is spent jumping on trampolines. We are too old for that, aren't we? We let go of Jell-O the same time we abandoned our Sandylion sticker collections and our Hypercolor T-shirts. Adults don't eat Jell-O, or if they do, they don't take it seriously. They are busy paying taxes, owning smartphones, and occasionally thinking about things like "good cholesterol versus bad cholesterol," "zero percent APR financing," and "chronic back pain." Adults meet people for games of racquetball, join book clubs, and take multivitamins that are not shaped like cartoon characters.

We are adults. Eating Jell-O is, traditionally, not something that adults do.

Except that, as we have discovered, day by day, through our grueling routines, sometimes being an adult is horrifically, mind-numbingly boring. Sometimes there are days when we want to put a fist through our office computers, tear up the paperwork we were supposed to be circulating, and run up to our boss, saying, "It's so nice today. Can we work outside?" There are days when it's beach-weather hot and we are trapped in an office with air-conditioning cold enough to give hypothermia to a penguin. There are days when, let's be honest, we are just not in the mood for a seven-dollar salad with chickpeas and carrot shavings, and if we eat another egg white omelet our souls will die. There are days when being an adult is so completely uninspiring that I would be totally okay with reverting to a childlike state and unapologetically slurping sweet, fruity Jell-O while jumping on a trampoline and holding a squirt gun full of lemonade.

We can't help growing up. But rather than leaving Jell-O behind as a fossilized relic of childhood, I decided to see if I could help it grow up as well. I wasn't about to make a tray of lime Jell-O, cut it into cubes, and put it out on a folding table next to a bunch of juice boxes. That wasn't what I wanted for something I remembered so fondly. Jell-O needed a makeover, badly, and I was ready for the challenge.

B.Y.O.J.

As a frequent guest at friends' dinner parties, I was tired of taking the requisite bottle of wine or hastily made brownies. I wanted to impress people, but no one was blown away by my ability to purchase a bottle of eight-dollar Merlot or floored by how adeptly I could buy cookies from the corner store. My unusual Jell-O molds not only impressed my friends and my friends' friends, they also fit the necessary three *I*'s:

Interesting ~ Inexpensive ~ Idiotproof

The first seems self-explanatory. The first time I took Jell-O to a party was the first time that something I had taken received so much attention. In a sea of cookies and pies, Jell-O molds get noticed at the dessert table. If you're adding liquor, they will get noticed even more quickly. (You can add a fourth *I* for Inebriating, if you are so inclined.) Rather than whipping up a batch of prepackaged watermelon Jell-O in a tin and sticking it next to a tray of plastic forks, I began creating my own flavor combinations: mint and watermelon, coconut and raspberry, chile and chocolate. I began adding cream or fresh fruit. I began layering, creating Jell-Os that are both opaque and translucent, creating Jell-Os with effervescent bubbles trapped in the gelatin, creating Jell-Os so brightly colored that they looked like those displays in modern art museums that people think are pretty but nobody completely understands.

The second is an issue for a lot of people—cost. I do not always have the money to purchase specialty ingredients. If I have a choice between paying my rent or spending fifty dollars on novelty groceries, I will pay my rent. Most of my Jell-O creations cost a few dollars at most. This allows me not only to keep a roof over my head but also to continue to enjoy electric lighting and indoor plumbing and to occasionally take a taxi home in the pouring rain. My Jell-Os are for people who want to create something visually striking but who would rather not pay four dollars for a single cupcake because, hey, those car payments aren't going to pay themselves.

As for the Jell-Os being idiotproof, I will say this about myself: although I am interested in cool ingredients and flavor combinations, I am not a trained chef. The Jell-O recipes here are for people who are creative and fun and are decent at following directions. Even if your highest culinary achievement was baking a cookie in an Easy-Bake oven using a 100-watt light bulb and you will never land a position on a cooking reality show, your experience—or lack of it— in no way prohibits you from trying any of the recipes in this book.

And if you feel comfortable working with Jell-O after attempting some of these recipes, feel free to get inventive and come up with some creations of your own.

THE BIRTH OF CREATIVE JELL-O

My love of creative Jell-Os grew out of my love of living in New York City, where everyone is mind-bogglingly creative. I am surrounded at all times by people who paint or draw or write or create fascinating graphics using their computers—people who sew their own clothing or work in interior design. In the midst of all this, I had hit a creative wall. Although I consider myself a creative person, my innovative streak had recently been limited to staging artistic photographs of my hamster. (While endearing, it was not as if I hoped to become the Ansel Adams of hamster photographers.) I wanted to create. I wanted to make something that I could share with others, and creating interesting Jell-Os helped fill that niche.

My first attempt at a creative Jell-O was simple: a vodka tonic with blueberries that I took to a friend's birthday. It featured a layer of Cool Whip and tonic, with a top layer of blueberries suspended in both vodka and lime Jell-O. Surrounded by other party guests, I slowly pulled off the mold to reveal my creation. And I was, admittedly, nervous. Arriving at an adult gathering with a container of Jell-O is like showing up at a child's birthday party and talking about the Dow Jones industrial average. People will think you're weird. Or so I thought. I looked at the people at the party with their designer eyeglasses and tasteful clothing, having conversations about art and business and work and life. I looked at the young urban professionals crowded into little groups, conversing over glasses of wine, and stood there with my Jell-O like a twelve-year-old, embarrassed and a little anxious.

And they loved it.

Everyone from the administrative assistants to the aspiring artists to the third-year, angst-ridden law students congregated around the Jell-O, asking what it was, what was in it, how I made it, how they could make it, and looking at it with the excitement and enthusiasm of kids being let out for recess. Since then I've made dozens of other Jell-O molds, experimenting with everything from green tea to tiramisu to eggnog made with creamy, dark rum. I've flavored them with spices and fruit juices, and folded in fresh produce, yogurt, and nuts. I've created luxuriously creamy molds and quirky alcoholic molds and gelatins based on holiday favorites and classic comfort foods. I've created Jell-Os for vegans, nonvegans, boozers, teetotalers, uptight perfectionists, laid-back hippies, young people, old people, and anyone in between. All of them have been both ogled and loved.

Because here's the thing: inside every adult with a seventy-dollar haircut is a little child smearing Vaseline in her hair, and inside every young professional enjoying an expensive dinner at a tapas bar is someone who would be just as happy marveling over a neon pink Jell-O mold shaped like a lobster in the cozy living room of a friend's apartment. And I'm not saying making a neon pink lobster Jell-O mold is appropriate for *all* occasions, because clearly it isn't. But we live in a world of gray pantsuits, office jobs, and dry conversations. If the adage "You are what you eat" is true, it's nice to see something brightly colored and resilient on the table.

TIPS, TRICKS, TOOLS, AND TECHNIQUES

MAKING YOUR GELATIN ISN'T ROCKET SCIENCE, but that's not to say you won't have questions. In my years of making creative Jell-Os, I've learned (often the hard way) what works and what doesn't. This tips and tricks chapter will give you the benefit of learning from my mistakes, answering questions about everything from refrigeration time to the perennial, why isn't it turning out like the picture?

How long should I refrigerate the gelatin?

Different gelatin recipes will require different techniques and refrigeration times. The consistency required for layering multiple gelatin flavors is different from the consistency required to immerse your coworker's stapler in Jell-O. On the opposite page is a guide to help achieve your mischievous gelatin needs. These times are approximate and will vary based on the volume of gelatin being used, the thickness of the layers being created, and the temperature of your refrigerator. It is best to check on the gelatin's consistency regularly during refrigeration.

Many of the recipes in this book call for unflavored gelatin rather than the fruit-flavored gelatin I am used to. What's the difference?

Unflavored gelatin, as the name suggests, is free of flavorings and sugar and therefore allows you to create a Jell-O mold "from scratch" using ingredients such as cream or fruit juices or even wine. It comes in powdered and sheet form, but for simplicity's sake, all of the recipes in this book call for the powdered form. Knox is the most common brand of unflavored gelatin and is typically sold in boxes of multiple envelopes containing 1/4 ounce each. Unflavored gelatin is also available in bulk, so all of the recipes in this book give gelatin amounts in both envelopes and tablespoons. Even though 1/4 ounce gelatin is actually slightly less than 1 tablespoon (that is, a "scant tablespoon"), I call for 1 tablespoon per package. That minor difference does not affect the recipe.

IF IT SAYS

REFRIGERATE UNTIL THICKENED	REFRIGERATE UNTIL SET BUT NOT FIRM	REFRIGERATE UNTIL FIRM
THE GELATIN SHOULD be the consistency of an extremely dense pudding.	**THE GELATIN SHOULD** stick to your finger if you touch it; if you tilt the mold, gelatin at this stage will tilt to the side.	**THE GELATIN SHOULD** not stick to your finger if you touch it; be immobile.
KEEP IT IN THE FRIDGE FOR approximately 1 hour and 30 minutes (depending on the volume, thickness, and chilling temperature).	**KEEP IT IN THE FRIDGE FOR** approximately 2 hours (depending on the volume, thickness, and chilling temperature).	**KEEP IT IN THE FRIDGE FOR** a minimum of 3 hours for individual molds, at least 4 hours for 2- to 6-cup molds, and at least 5 hours or overnight for 8- to 12-cup molds.
YOU NEED IT LIKE THIS SO YOU CAN suspend fruit, vegetables, gummy sharks, or your roommate's car keys in the gelatin.	**YOU NEED IT LIKE THIS SO YOU CAN** layer different flavors of gelatin and have them stick together.	**YOU NEED IT LIKE THIS SO YOU CAN** put it in the fridge, watch the *Lord of the Rings* trilogy (it'll be done by the time Frodo leaves Middle-earth for the Undying Lands), take it out of the mold, and eat it. Serve it to friends at a party or eat it alone in your bathrobe. It's your call.

I've never seen a store that sells Jell-O molds. Are molds necessary? Where can I find them?

Jell-O is a lot like wedding cake: you want it to taste good, but people also pay attention to how it looks. Rather than pouring your gelatin into an empty Chinese food container, invest in some interesting molds. Websites like eBay and Etsy sell vintage copper molds. If, like me, you have relatives who just can't seem to stay away from Salvation Army stores, you can find them there as well. You can use molds intended for soaps or candies, decorative Bundt cake pans, loaf pans, metal mixing bowls, or quirky ice-cube trays. For my very first Jell-O mold masterpiece, I used a Tupperware container—no frills, but it got the job done. Consider picking up holiday- or occasion-themed molds based on specific Jell-Os you want to try: a wreath-shaped mold for Christmas, a heart-shaped mold for Valentine's Day. You don't want to show up on St. Patrick's Day with a mold shaped like a dreidel, and you certainly don't want to prepare for your niece's birthday with the same mold you used for your friend's bachelorette party.

What size mold will I need?

Most of the recipes in this book fill a 4- to 6-cup mold, but occasionally there'll be something larger, so keep at least one large mold on hand. Bundt cake pans that hold 8 to 10 cups will work. Individual molds should have a capacity of $1/2$ to $3/4$ cup.

How the %&@# do you get it out of the mold?

....

This is one of the questions most frequently asked by beginners. Many a novice has worked hard to create the perfect Jell-O mold, only to stare blankly at the gelatin in its container, having no idea how to get it out, looking for a zipper or pull-tab or eject button. Don't lose any sleep over this. Getting your gelatin out of the mold is simple.

1. MAKE SURE YOUR GELATIN IS FIRM, using the table on page 9 as a guide.

2. MOISTEN THE TIPS OF YOUR FINGERS and gently pull the edges of the gelatin away from the mold.

3. DIP THE MOLD IN WARM (NOT HOT) WATER. Immerse it so the water comes up to, but not over, the rim. Keep submerged for 15 seconds.

4. MOISTEN A SERVING PLATE (so you can slide your mold and center it on the plate once unmolded) and place it upside down over the mold.

5. HOLD THE MOLD AND THE PLATE TOGETHER, invert, shake slightly to loosen the gelatin, then carefully pull the mold away. (If this does not work, repeat the steps.)

6. TA-DA!

It's taking FOR-EV-ER. Can't I make it chill faster somehow?

Yes.

1. **THE CONTAINER YOU USE AFFECTS HOW QUICKLY THE MOLD WILL CHILL.** Metal bowls or molds will get cold faster and your gelatin will be ready in less time.

2. **SIZE IS ALSO A CONSIDERATION.** A dozen small Jell-O molds will be ready much sooner than one enormous mother-ship-size Jell-O mold. Using individual molds can cut a few hours off your chilling time.

3. **THE ICE-BATH METHOD.** Prepare the gelatin per the recipe. Place the bowl of gelatin mixture in a large bowl of ice and water. Stir the mixture occasionally as it chills to ensure it retains a smooth consistency as it thickens.

So I'm trying to make a layered mold and none of the layers are sticking together. Please help me before I start crying.

Layered molds can be a little tricky, but success comes with patience. Follow these steps and it should turn out beautifully. If one layer is too firm, the layer placed on top will slide right off it. Conversely, if one layer is too soft, the colors will blend together.

1. **REFRIGERATE EACH LAYER UNTIL SET BUT NOT FIRM** (see the table on page 9) before adding the next layer.

2. **WITH THE EXCEPTION OF THE FIRST LAYER,** make sure the gelatin mixtures for subsequent layers have cooled and thickened a little before adding. If

you pour the gelatin mixture while it is still warm, it may "melt" the previous layer a bit, causing the flavors and colors to run together.

3. **ALSO, AS YOU WILL NEED TO WAIT FOR ABOUT AN HOUR** (depending on the thickness of the layers) for each of the layers in a layered mold to solidify, use the down time productively. It's an excellent excuse to clean your living room, take up calligraphy, catch up on episodes of whatever show everyone at your workplace "can't stop talking about," learn a new language, or feed your hamster.

Can I have a list of common mistakes people have made with their Jell-O molds so that I can avoid making those same mistakes?

You most certainly may have one of those lists.

It's getting all clumpy! Why is it getting all clumpy?!

To avoid clumping when using unflavored gelatin, sprinkle the gelatin over cold water and allow the granules to partially hydrate for 2 to 4 minutes before adding the hot water. (This step is included in all of the recipes that use unflavored gelatin.)

Why does my gelatin have little pieces of purple sand in it?

To make sure flavored gelatin is clear and evenly set, check that all the granules are completely dissolved in boiling water or other liquid before adding the cold liquid.

What happens if I leave my unmolded gelatin out on the counter overnight?

If you're storing a gelatin mold overnight, keep it in the refrigerator. Unless you used a mold shaped like the Wicked Witch of the West, you're not going to be a big fan of the "I'm melting" look.

I left it in the fridge overnight and it's so dry it looks like it should be in a commercial for moisturizer. How can I prevent this?

If you're storing the gelatin in its mold overnight, cover it with plastic wrap to prevent it from drying out.

Is Jell-O one of those things you can make today and then eat three years from now?

No, that is a terrible idea. Gelatin is best if eaten within three days of making it. Don't try to freeze your Jell-O mold either. The water and the other ingredients will separate and it will turn to a slushy mess.

I'm having trouble evenly mixing in some of the creamy ingredients.

If you're mixing sour cream, yogurt, or mayonnaise into your gelatin, use a fork or a wire whisk rather than a spoon.

I'm trying to add fresh pineapple and kiwi to my Jell-O and something is going horribly, abysmally wrong.

Fresh or frozen pineapple, kiwi, figs, guava, ginger, and papaya contain an enzyme that breaks down gelatin, preventing it from thickening. Cooking deactivates this enzyme, so canned versions are fine. If you want to use fresh pineapple, simply slice or dice the pineapple per the instructions in the recipe and boil it in water to cover for 10 minutes. Drain the water and let the pineapple cool to room temperature before adding it to your gelatin mixture.

It's taking longer than usual for all of the gelatin granules to dissolve in the milk. Is that normal?

Yep. Gelatin can sometimes take a little longer when used with cream or milk.

Happy Jell-O-ing!

SUSPENDED FRUIT
AND MORE!

*I*T'S FUN TO SUSPEND THINGS IN JELL-O. But while you may be excited to drop in your grandfather's fake teeth or your boyfriend's glasses, this book (disappointingly, I'm sorry) will deal mainly with adding fruit. Give your gelatin the funky look of suspended animation with these nontraditional salads. Once you've mastered the technique, feel free to either create a recipe of your own, or for those who are more mischievous and less culinary, make a beautiful creation composed of fruit juice, gelatin, and your mother's credit cards.

pomegranate berry salad

Makes one 6-cup gelatin mold

This summery pomegranate mold is both sweet and tart with bursts of berry flavor. And according to most advertisements for pomegranate juice, this *wunder*-fruit will prevent cancer, increase blood flow to the heart, lower cholesterol, and stave off arthritis, heart disease, and premature aging. While I was thinking of putting together a penicillin Jell-O or a smallpox-vaccine gelatin, this seems just as beneficial and is probably much tastier. For the berries, I recommend a mix of blueberries, raspberries, and blackberries, but you can substitute any berries that are in season. For extra zip, try substituting vodka for half of the ginger ale or tonic.

2 tablespoons (2 envelopes) unflavored gelatin powder

1/4 cup cold water

2 cups boiling pomegranate juice

1 1/2 cups cold ginger ale or tonic water

2 cups mixed fresh berries

IN A BOWL, sprinkle the gelatin evenly over the water and allow the gelatin to absorb the water for 2 minutes. Add the boiling pomegranate juice to the gelatin mixture and stir until the gelatin is fully dissolved. Stir in the ginger ale and refrigerate until thickened (see page 9). Fold in the berries and spoon into a 6-cup mold. Refrigerate until firm (see page 9). Unmold and serve.

cheery cherry salad

Makes one 6-cup gelatin mold

Life is just a bowl of cherries. This delicious mold, packed with sweet cherries, cherry cola, and brandy, is perfect for the perennial optimist. (It can be served to pessimists as well, though with mixed results.) This recipe is great on its own, but to make it extra fancy, serve it in your own homemade chocolate dessert cups (make a double batch of the Chocolate Cups on page 37). Note: You must marinate the cherries in brandy for 24 hours, so be sure to plan ahead.

2 cups pitted fresh or frozen and thawed dark sweet cherries

1/2 cup brandy, or more if needed

2 tablespoons (2 envelopes) unflavored gelatin powder

1/2 cup cold water

1/2 cup boiling water

1/2 cup sugar

2 cups cherry cola

BEFORE PREPARING THE GELATIN RECIPE, marinate 1 cup of the cherries in enough brandy to cover them (at least 1/2 cup) for 24 hours. Drain the cherries, reserving the brandy.

In a large bowl, sprinkle the gelatin evenly over the cold water and allow the gelatin to absorb the water for 2 minutes. Add the boiling water to the gelatin mixture and stir until the gelatin is fully dissolved. Stir in the sugar, cola, and 1/2 cup of the brandy used to marinate the cherries. Refrigerate until thickened (see page 9). Fold in the marinated and plain cherries and spoon into a 6-cup mold. Refrigerate until firm (see page 9). Unmold and serve.

million dollar gelatin

Makes one 5-cup gelatin mold

This inexplicably named Jell-O mold is based on the recipe for the inexplicably named pie. It does not contain actual money, but it is rich in creamy, pineapple-y flavor. Remember to use canned pineapple (or if it's fresh or frozen, boil it for 10 minutes first) or the gelatin won't firm up.

2 tablespoons (2 envelopes) unflavored gelatin powder

1/2 cup cold water

1/2 cup boiling water

1 (8-ounce) tub frozen whipped topping, thawed

1 cup sweetened condensed milk

1 cup drained canned crushed pineapple

1/2 cup chopped pecans

IN A LARGE BOWL, sprinkle the gelatin evenly over the cold water and allow the gelatin to absorb the water for 2 minutes. Add the boiling water to the gelatin mixture and stir until the gelatin is fully dissolved. Stir in the whipped topping and sweetened condensed milk and beat with a wire whisk until the mixture is smooth. Refrigerate until thickened (see page 9). Fold in the pineapple and pecans and spoon into a 5-cup mold. Refrigerate until firm (see page 9). Unmold and serve.

carrot cake

Makes one 4-cup gelatin mold

If carrots are good for your eyes, this Jell-O will save you a trip to the ophthal-mologist. This dual-layer gelatin features an amberlike layer of carrots mixed with the warm flavors of vanilla and cinnamon and is topped off with a layer of carroty cream cheese. And I don't know if pecans are supposed to be good for your eyes, but what the heck, let's throw them in too. The orange-carrot juice for this recipe comes bottled and can be obtained at most any grocery store.

First Layer

1 tablespoon (1 envelope) unflavored gelatin powder

1/2 cup cold orange-carrot juice

1/2 cup boiling water

1/4 cup sugar

1 cup (8-ounce brick) cream cheese, very soft room temperature

TO MAKE THE FIRST LAYER, in a bowl, sprinkle the gelatin evenly over the cold orange-carrot juice and allow the gelatin to absorb the juice for 2 minutes. Add the boiling water and stir until the gelatin is fully dissolved. Add the sugar and stir until fully dissolved. Beat in the cream cheese with an electric mixer until the mixture is smooth. Spoon into a 4-cup mold. Refrigerate until the gelatin is set but not firm (see page 9). Note: This layer may begin to set faster than the next layer can be prepared, so it may be best to leave it at room temperature until the next layer is nearly ready. If the first layer does begin to set faster than the second layer can be prepared, dip the mold into a pan of hot water to slow the setting. Alternatively, reheat the carrot juice

CONTINUED

carrot cake,
continued

Second Layer

1 tablespoon (1 envelope) unflavored gelatin powder

1/2 cup cold orange-carrot juice

1 cup boiling orange-carrot juice

1/2 cup sugar

1 teaspoon vanilla extract

1/2 teaspoon ground cinnamon

1/2 cup finely grated, peeled carrots

1/2 cup chopped pecans or walnuts

and cream cheese mixture in a saucepan until softened, pour it back into the mold, and wait for it to become set but not firm.

Meanwhile, to make the second layer, in a separate bowl, sprinkle the gelatin evenly over the cold orange-carrot juice and allow the gelatin to absorb the juice for 2 minutes. Add the boiling orange-carrot juice and stir until the gelatin is fully dissolved. Stir in the sugar, then the vanilla and cinnamon. Refrigerate until thickened (see page 9). Fold in the carrots and pecans. Gently spoon the mixture into the mold over the cream cheese layer. Refrigerate until firm (see page 9). Unmold and serve.

nut 'n' honey

Makes one 5-cup gelatin mold

This earthy gelatin combines brown sugar, almonds, pecans, and oats and encases the mixture in honey for a hearty, natural feel—like a granola bar but without the crumbly mess. Note: This recipe is best served fresh, lest the nuts lose their crunch and the sugar in the honey starts to break down.

1/2 cup rolled oats

1/2 cup silvered almonds

1/2 cup crushed pecans

1/2 cup firmly packed dark brown sugar

2 tablespoons pure maple syrup

2 tablespoons (2 envelopes) unflavored gelatin powder

1/2 cup cold water

2 1/4 cups boiling water

2/3 cup honey

1 teaspoon vanilla extract

PREHEAT THE OVEN TO 300°F. Line a baking sheet with parchment paper. In a bowl, mix together the oats, almonds, pecans, brown sugar, and maple syrup. Spread the mixture over the prepared baking sheet. Bake for 15 minutes. Let the mixture cool to room temperature.

In a separate bowl, sprinkle the gelatin evenly over the cold water and allow the gelatin to absorb the water for 2 minutes. Add the boiling water and stir until the gelatin is fully dissolved. Add the honey and vanilla and stir until the honey has fully liquefied. Refrigerate until thickened (see page 9). Fold in the oat mixture and spoon into a 5-cup mold. Refrigerate until firm (see page 9). Unmold and serve.

orange spice

Makes one 6-cup gelatin mold

This Jell-O is so reminiscent of autumn that the mere scent of it makes me want to buy school supplies. Combine some of fall's favorite spices, rich orange gelatin, and a little vinegar for something that will be sweet, tangy, and the perfect reward for anyone who spent upward of four hours raking leaves. For the peaches and syrup, you can either use canned peaches in heavy syrup or fresh peaches and bottled peach nectar.

3/4 cup heavy peach syrup (from canned peaches, below) or peach nectar

1/4 cup distilled white vinegar

1/2 cup sugar

12 whole cloves

1/8 teaspoon ground cinnamon

1 (16-ounce) can peaches in heavy syrup, drained and chopped, or 2 cups peeled, pitted, and chopped fresh peaches

2 (3-ounce) packages orange-flavored gelatin

1 1/2 cups boiling water

3/4 cup light rum

IN A SAUCEPAN, stir together the peach syrup, vinegar, sugar, cloves, and cinnamon and bring to a boil over medium heat. Add the peaches, decrease the heat to low, and simmer for 5 minutes. Remove from the heat and discard the cloves.

Meanwhile, in a bowl, add the gelatin to the boiling water and stir until the gelatin is fully dissolved. Whisk into the peach mixture. Stir in the rum. Let the mixture cool to room temperature and pour into a 6-cup mold. Refrigerate until firm (see page 9). Unmold and serve.

CREAMY AND DREAMY

WHENEVER THERE'S AN AD ON TELEVISION for something delicious and creamy, the announcer's voice becomes smooth and deep to the point where you wonder if you're watching a commercial for ice cream or a late-night Cinemax movie. The addition of cream takes gelatin from refreshing to sumptuous. From a rich, indulgent crème brûlée to a healthy lemon–poppy seed yogurt, these molds add a new dimension to Jell-O. Suddenly a happy-go-lucky dessert becomes something much more substantial and decadent. These molds exude indulgence. They work well as individual molds for large dinner parties or, if no one else is around, for eating under cashmere throws while curled up next to the fireplace, with well-groomed purebred dogs on handwoven oriental carpets at your feet.

green milk tea

Makes one 4-cup gelatin mold or 4 or 5 individual molds

The creamy simplicity of blueberries folded into green tea ice cream is the Jell-O equivalent of a yoga class. We're not saying this gelatin itself is relaxing, but have you ever seen anyone drinking green tea, eating blueberries, and looking stressed? Yeah, neither have I. This recipe is cute served in small, clear juice glasses like minicups of green bubble tea.

2 tablespoons (2 envelopes) unflavored gelatin powder

1/2 cup cold water

3/4 cup boiling whole or 2 percent milk

1/2 cup sugar

2 cups (1 pint) green tea ice cream, at room temperature

1/2 cup fresh or frozen and thawed blueberries

IN A BOWL, sprinkle the gelatin evenly over the cold water and allow the gelatin to absorb the water for 2 minutes. Add the boiling milk and stir until the gelatin is fully dissolved. Add the sugar and stir until fully dissolved. Add the ice cream and stir until the mixture is smooth. Refrigerate until thickened (see page 9). Fold in the blueberries and spoon into a 4-cup mold or 4 or 5 small, clear glasses. Refrigerate until firm (see page 9). Unmold and serve, or serve in the glasses.

lemon poppy seed

Makes one 4-cup gelatin mold

When life gives you lemons, make lemonade. But if life gives you lemons and poppy seeds and yogurt and a cup of boiling water and a packet of unflavored gelatin, clearly, life is trying to tell you something *very specific*. This simple recipe is the perfect combination of sweet and tart. If life doesn't hand you each of the ingredients, you can obviously just go out and buy them. I use yellow food coloring for a more vibrant color. If you want to go that extra step, spring for organic plant-based yellow food dye—it's more natural than Yellow No. 5.

2 tablespoons (2 envelopes) unflavored gelatin powder

1/2 cup cold water

1 cup boiling water

3/4 cup sugar

3/4 cup freshly squeezed or bottled lemon juice

1 cup plain yogurt

4 drops yellow food coloring (optional)

1 teaspoon poppy seeds

IN A BOWL, sprinkle the gelatin evenly over the cold water and allow the gelatin to absorb the water for 2 minutes. Add the boiling water and stir until the gelatin is fully dissolved. Add the sugar and stir until fully dissolved.

In a separate bowl, whisk the lemon juice and yogurt together until the mixture is smooth. Whisk the yogurt mixture into the gelatin mixture. Blend in the yellow food coloring, stirring until a uniform color. Refrigerate until thickened (see page 9). Fold in the poppy seeds and spoon into a 4-cup mold. Refrigerate until firm (see page 9). Unmold and serve.

key lime pie

The word *Florida* has become synonymous with alligator-filled swamps, droves of shuffleboard-playing senior citizens, and vast amusement-park empires. But the state is also famous for the sweet simplicity of its Key lime pie. This tangy, layered Jell-O is the best thing about Florida since the Everglades. When zesting the limes, take care to remove only the vibrant green zest, not the bitter white pith beneath. Depending on the circumference of the mold, it may be necessary to double the recipe for the crust layer to cover the Key lime layer completely.

Key Lime Layer

2 tablespoons (2 envelopes) unflavored gelatin powder

1/2 cup cold water

1/2 cup boiling water

1¼ cups (14-ounce can) sweetened condensed milk

1 cup bottled or freshly squeezed Key lime juice

1 tablespoon freshly grated lime zest (from 3 to 5 limes)

1/2 cup sour cream

1 drop green food coloring (optional)

TO MAKE THE FIRST LAYER, in a bowl, sprinkle the gelatin evenly over the cold water and allow the gelatin to absorb the water for 2 minutes. Add the boiling water and stir until the gelatin is fully dissolved. Whisk in the sweetened condensed milk, lime juice, lime zest, sour cream, and food coloring until the mixture is smooth. Spoon into a 6-cup mold. Refrigerate until the gelatin is set but not firm (see page 9). Note: This layer may begin to set faster than the crust layer can be prepared, so it may be best to leave it at room temperature until the next layer is nearly ready. If the first layer does begin to set faster than the second layer can be prepared, dip the mold into a pan of hot water to slow the setting. Alternatively, reheat the

CONTINUED

Crust Layer

1 tablespoon (1 envelope) unflavored gelatin powder

3/4 cup cold milk

1 1/2 cups crushed graham crackers

Key lime mixture in a saucepan until softened, pour it back into the mold, and wait for it to become set but not firm.

To make the second layer, in a saucepan, sprinkle the gelatin evenly over the cold milk and allow the gelatin to absorb the milk for 2 minutes. Bring the milk just to a boil over medium heat, being careful not to let the milk boil over. Remove from the heat. Allow the gelatin mixture to cool to room temperature; stir in the graham cracker crumbs. Gently spoon into the mold over the Key lime layer. Refrigerate until firm (see page 9). Unmold and serve.

creamsicle

Makes one 5-cup gelatin mold

This orange creamsicle mold is everything nostalgic about summers at the neighborhood pool snack bar. And with fresh orange juice, vanilla ice cream, and mandarin oranges, it's better than those artificially flavored pops from the frozen-food aisle. For best results, pair this mold with a public pool, a watch tan, and a seventeen-year-old lifeguard telling you there's no running next to the diving boards.

2 tablespoons (2 envelopes) unflavored gelatin powder

1/2 cup cold water

1 1/2 cups boiling orange juice

1 1/2 cups vanilla ice cream, at room temperature

2 cups drained canned mandarin orange slices

IN A BOWL, sprinkle the gelatin evenly over the cold water and allow the gelatin to absorb the water for 2 minutes. Add the boiling orange juice and stir until the gelatin is fully dissolved. Add the ice cream and stir until the mixture is smooth. Refrigerate until thickened (see page 9), stirring occasionally to keep the mixture smooth, as the ice cream may start to separate from the orange juice. Fold in the mandarin oranges and spoon into a 5-cup mold. Refrigerate until firm (see page 9). Unmold and serve.

chocolate raspberry mousse cups

Makes 6 dessert cups

As soon as a dessert involves something served in a chocolate cup, it has my undivided attention. This fabulous dessert crosses indulgent chocolate with a filling of light, fruity raspberry mousse. Individual servings are perfect for sharing. (Or, if you're so inclined, not sharing.) You can garnish these little gems with whipped cream and chocolate shavings, or a couple of jaunty raspberries, if you like. Refrigerate any extra mousse in a separate container to snack on later.

Chocolate Cups

2 cups semisweet chocolate chips

2 tablespoons solid vegetable shortening

Raspberry Mousse

1 tablespoon (1 envelope) unflavored gelatin powder

1/4 cup cold water

1/2 cup boiling water

1/4 cup sugar

1 1/2 cups fresh raspberries

2 cups whipped cream (1 cup heavy cream, whipped)

TO MAKE THE CHOCOLATE CUPS, in a small saucepan, heat the chocolate chips and shortening over high heat, stirring continuously until melted. Using the back of a metal spoon, spread the chocolate evenly inside six 3 1/2-inch foil muffin liners. Refrigerate until firm, about 30 minutes.

To make the mousse, in a bowl, sprinkle the gelatin evenly over the cold water and allow the gelatin to absorb the water for 2 minutes. Add the boiling water and stir until the gelatin is fully dissolved. Add the sugar and stir until dissolved. Transfer the gelatin mixture to a blender. Add the berries and blend until liquefied. Set a fine-mesh strainer over a bowl and pour the mixture through the strainer to strain out the seeds. Refrigerate until thickened (see page 9).

CONTINUED

chocolate raspberry mousse cups,
continued

Rinse the blender of any remaining raspberry seeds and return the thickened raspberry gelatin mixture to the blender. Add the whipped cream and blend until smooth. Refrigerate until thickened (see page 9).

Carefully peel away the foil from the chocolate cups. Spoon the mousse into the cups and serve.

apricot cream

Makes one 4-cup gelatin mold

The apricot hails from the cradle of civilization—the Tigris-Euphrates River Valley—and has been popular in that area for thousands of years. Enjoy a fruit that's been around since the dawn of history, immersed in a Jell-O as monumental as the discovery of agriculture or language. (Okay, not quite. But for what it is, it's delicious.)

1/2 cup dried apricots

2 tablespoons (2 envelopes) unflavored gelatin powder

1/2 cup cold water

3/4 cup boiling water

1 cup sweetened condensed milk

1 cup apricot nectar

PLACE THE APRICOTS IN A SAUCEPAN, add enough water to cover the fruit, and bring to a boil over high heat. Decrease heat to medium-low and simmer for 7 minutes, until the apricots are tender. With a slotted spoon, remove the apricots from the pan, letting any water drain away, and place in a bowl. Mash them until there are no large chunks; reserve.

Meanwhile, in a bowl, sprinkle the gelatin evenly over the cold water and allow the gelatin to absorb the water for 2 minutes. Add the boiling water and stir until the gelatin is fully dissolved. Pour in the sweetened condensed milk and apricot nectar, and stir until the mixture is smooth. Refrigerate until thickened (see page 9). Stir in the mashed apricots and spoon into a 4-cup mold. Refrigerate until firm (see page 9). Unmold and serve.

crème brûlée

Makes one 3-cup gelatin mold or 4 to 6 ramekins

If you're one of those people who loves the rich taste of crème brûlée but doesn't own a tiny blowtorch, or whatever it is they use to caramelize the sugar on those things, may I humbly suggest this Jell-O mold—all of the rich creamy taste with none of the fire hazard.

1 tablespoon (1 envelope) unflavored gelatin powder

1/4 cup cold water

2 cups heavy cream

1/3 cup granulated sugar

1 heaping tablespoon dark brown sugar

1 teaspoon vanilla extract

IN A BOWL, sprinkle the gelatin evenly over the cold water and allow the gelatin to absorb the water for 2 minutes.

Meanwhile, in a saucepan, bring the cream just to a boil over medium heat, being careful not to let the cream boil over. Remove from the heat. Pour the boiling cream into the bowl with the gelatin and stir until gelatin is fully dissolved into the cream.

Add the granulated sugar, brown sugar, and vanilla and stir until smooth. Let the mixture cool to room temperature. Pour into a 3-cup mold or 4 to 6 ramekins. Refrigerate until firm (see page 9). Unmold and serve, or serve in the ramekins.

chai tea panna cotta

Makes 4 individual molds

This indulgent recipe is perfect for a winter's day, and particularly adorable served in little tea cups. Mixing the richness of cream with the warm variety of spices in chai, consider this your Jell-O reward for shoveling the four feet of snow that seem to continually accumulate on the driveway in January. Winter is the perfect time for delicious extravagances. Note: The recipe is more custardy and calls for less gelatin than a typical mold. Therefore, take great care when unmolding this treat.

1¼ cups milk

1¼ cups heavy cream

½ cup sugar

3 chai tea bags, or 1 tablespoon plus 1 teaspoon loose chai tea in a tea infuser

1 tablespoon (1 envelope) unflavored gelatin powder

¼ cup cold water

IN A LARGE SAUCEPAN, bring the milk, cream, and sugar just to a boil over medium heat, being careful not to let the liquid boil over. Add the tea and simmer for 10 minutes. Remove from the heat, remove and discard the tea bags, and reserve.

Meanwhile, in a bowl, sprinkle the gelatin evenly over the cold water and allow the gelatin to absorb the water for 2 minutes. Pour the reserved chai milk mixture into the bowl with the gelatin and stir until the gelatin is fully dissolved into the milk. Let the mixture cool to room temperature. Pour into 4 individual molds or teacups. Refrigerate until firm (see page 9). Unmold and serve, or serve in the teacups.

grasshopper pie

Makes one 6-cup gelatin mold (or one 8-cup mold if the crust layer is doubled)

Crumbled chocolate cookies and delicious crème de menthe give the color and texture to this classic dessert derived from a cocktail that has (thank goodness) nothing at all to do with actual grasshoppers. Note: If you are short on time, you can chill the crème de menthe ahead of time (I keep all my booze in the freezer anyhow) and the layer will set faster. For a paler, minty-looking color for your finished mold, use clear crème de menthe and a few drops of green food dye, rather than the precolored liqueur. Depending on the circumference of the mold, it may be necessary to double the recipe for the crust layer to cover the grasshopper layer completely.

Grasshopper Layer

2 tablespoons (2 envelopes) unflavored gelatin powder

1/2 cup cold water

1/2 cup boiling water

1 1/4 cups (14-ounce can) sweetened condensed milk

1 1/2 cups crème de menthe

1/2 cup sour cream

3 or 4 drops green food coloring, if using clear crème de menthe

TO MAKE THE FIRST LAYER, in a bowl, sprinkle the gelatin evenly over the cold water and allow the gelatin to absorb the water for 2 minutes. Add the boiling water and stir until the gelatin is fully dissolved. Whisk in the sweetened condensed milk, crème de menthe, sour cream, and food coloring until the mixture is smooth. Spoon into a 6-cup mold. Refrigerate until the mixture is set but not firm (see page 9). Note: This layer may begin to set faster than the next layer can be prepared, so it may be best to leave it at room temperature until the next layer is nearly ready. If the first

CONTINUED

Crust Layer

1 tablespoon (1 envelope) unflavored gelatin powder

3/4 cup cold whole or 2 percent milk

1 1/2 cups crushed chocolate cookies

layer does begin to set faster than the second layer can be prepared, dip the mold into a pan of hot water to slow the setting. Alternatively, reheat the grasshopper mixture in a saucepan until softened, pour it back into the mold, and wait for it to become set but not firm.

To make the second layer, in a large saucepan, sprinkle the gelatin evenly over the cold milk and allow the gelatin to absorb the milk for 2 minutes. Bring the mixture just to a boil over medium-low heat, being careful not to let the milk boil over. Remove from the heat and let cool to room temperature. Stir in the chocolate cookie crumbs. Gently spoon into the mold over the crème de menthe layer. Refrigerate until firm (see page 9). Unmold and serve.

BOOZY MOLDS

FROM MY BEAUTIFUL WHITE SANGRIA GELATIN to the mimosa, mojito, and piña colada molds, Jell-O is a wonderful way to enjoy drinks and dessert at the same time. Rather than showing up at a party with a six-dollar box of wine or beer in a brown-paper bag, take one of these creative Jell-Os that can be food, drink, and topic of conversation in one jiggly package. You love the idea of serving an alcoholic Jell-O but don't want your dinner gathering to seem too much like an out-of-control frat party? These gelatins punch up the fun without making you feel like you're a twenty-one-year-old drinking to avoid finishing a term paper. Think of these as the "modern-art" version of Jell-O shots.

mimosa

Makes one 4-cup gelatin mold

Brunch, that magical meal that allows you to freely eat French toast or eggs Benedict at three thirty in the afternoon without explanation or regret, cannot be considered complete without the addition of a mimosa. A tangy mix of orange juice and sparkling champagne, this gelatin will perk up your spirits, satisfy your taste buds, and help get a strong, albeit belated, start to the day. For an extra flourish, chill and serve the gelatin in widemouthed champagne glasses with long, narrow spoons. Note: Don't be cheap. This recipe will really pop with freshly squeezed orange juice and good-quality champagne.

2 tablespoons (2 envelopes) unflavored gelatin powder

1/2 cup cold water

1 1/2 cups boiling freshly squeezed orange juice

2 cups cold champagne

IN A BOWL, sprinkle the gelatin evenly over the cold water and allow the gelatin to absorb the water for 2 minutes. Add the boiling orange juice and stir until the gelatin is fully dissolved. Stir in the champagne. Let cool to room temperature. Pour into a 4-cup mold. Refrigerate until firm (see page 9). Unmold and serve.

white sangria

Makes one 6-cup gelatin mold

Another Jell-O invented with a warm-weather party in mind. The sweet, fruity taste of white sangria involves grapes, apples, and strawberries suspended in a delicious blend of apple juice and white wine. Wear those white linen pants or just throw on sunglasses and a loose shirt. No dress code. The fun begins when you put this sangria-inspired mold on the table. For a sweeter sangria, use a sweeter white wine.

2 tablespoons (2 envelopes) unflavored gelatin powder

1/2 cup cold water

1 1/2 cups boiling apple juice

1 1/2 cups cold white wine

1 cup sliced fresh strawberries

1 cup grapes, halved

1 cup diced apple

IN A BOWL, sprinkle the gelatin evenly over the cold water and allow the gelatin to absorb the water for 2 minutes. Add the boiling apple juice and stir until the gelatin is fully dissolved. Stir in the wine. Refrigerate until thickened (see page 9). Fold in the strawberries, grapes, and apples. Spoon into a 6-cup mold. Refrigerate until firm (see page 9). Unmold and serve.

sparkling champagne and strawberries

Makes 7 to 10 individual molds or one 7-cup gelatin mold

Pop open a bottle of champagne! Whether it's used to welcome the New Year, toast the bride and groom, or pour over bikini-clad women in a music video, champagne is a sign that something special is going on. This celebratory gelatin encases fresh ripe strawberries in effervescent layers of clear bubbles. To get the full champagne glass effect, mold the gelatin in tall cups—just make sure, for unmolding purposes, that the opening is wider than the base.

3 tablespoons (3 envelopes) unflavored gelatin powder

2 cups cold water

1 cup sugar

1¹/₂ cups cold champagne

1¹/₂ cups cold ginger ale

1 cup sliced fresh strawberries

IN A SAUCEPAN, sprinkle the gelatin evenly over the cold water and allow the gelatin to absorb the water for 2 minutes. Bring the water to a boil over high heat and stir until the gelatin is fully dissolved. Remove from the heat.

Transfer the gelatin mixture to a bowl, add the sugar, and stir until dissolved. Stir in the champagne and ginger ale. Refrigerate until thickened (see page 9). Fold in the strawberries and spoon into 7 to 10 individual molds or a 7-cup mold. Refrigerate until firm (see page 9). Unmold and serve.

mojito

Makes one 3-cup gelatin mold

A lot of great things come out of Cuba, but encasing illegal cigars or roast pork and Swiss cheese sandwiches in gelatin and serving them at a party doesn't cut it. Hence, the mojito. The staple of every competent bartender becomes the highlight of a dinner gathering. Note: The more you like the flavor of mint, the longer you can simmer the mint in this recipe.

1 cup fresh mint leaves, plus 6 to 8 leaves for garnish

1/2 cup sugar

1 1/2 cups cold water

2 tablespoons (2 envelopes) unflavored gelatin powder

1 cup tonic water

3/4 cup light rum

1 tablespoon lime juice

IN A SAUCEPAN, bring the mint leaves, sugar, and 1 cup of the water to a boil over high heat. Decrease the heat to low and simmer for 2 minutes, stirring occasionally. Strain out the mint leaves.

Meanwhile, in a bowl, sprinkle the gelatin evenly over the remaining 1/2 cup cold water and allow the gelatin to absorb the water for 2 minutes. Add the boiling mint-infused liquid and stir until the gelatin is fully dissolved. Let the mixture cool; stir in the tonic, rum, and lime juice. Refrigerate until thickened (see page 9). Stir the thickened gelatin to create bubbles. Spoon a small amount into a 3-cup mold. Arrange the mint leaves for garnish in a pattern over the gelatin in the mold, then gently spoon the remaining gelatin into the mold. Refrigerate until firm (see page 9). Unmold and serve.

piña colada

Makes one 4-cup gelatin mold

If you like booze in your Jell-O, and getting caught in the rain
If you're not into yoga, if you have half a brain . . .

If you know the rest of the lyrics, feel free to keep singing. And if you have a pantry stocked with rum, pineapple, and coconut milk, get to work on this one and throw a party for your half-brained, yoga-hating, rain-soaked friends. Remember to use canned pineapple (or if it's fresh or frozen, boil it for 10 minutes first) or the gelatin won't firm up.

2 cups boiling water

2 (3-ounce) packages pineapple-flavored gelatin

3/4 cup cold coconut milk

3/4 cup cold spiced rum

6 or 7 canned or boiled pineapple rings (see headnote)

3 or 4 maraschino cherries, drained and halved

IN A BOWL, add the boiling water to the gelatin and stir until fully dissolved. Pour in the coconut milk and rum and stir until fully incorporated. Refrigerate until thickened (see page 9).

Meanwhile, drain the canned pineapple rings and press out more of the moisture between 2 paper towels. Arrange the rings on the bottom of a fairly flat 4-cup mold or pineapple upside-down pan. Place a cherry half, cut side up, in the center of each pineapple ring.

Gently spoon the thickened gelatin into the mold over the pineapple rings. Refrigerate until firm (see page 9). Unmold and serve.

pear and lychee martini

Makes one 5-cup gelatin mold or 6 to 10 individual glasses

Here's a sophisticated downtown taste that won't spill when enjoyed in a martini glass. Because really? We can put a man on the moon but we can't design a more practical glass in which to serve highly alcoholic beverages? While you bemoan our society's technological imperfections, enjoy ripe pear juice mixed with fresh lychees. And, of course, vodka.

2 tablespoons (2 envelopes) unflavored gelatin powder

1/2 cup cold water

1 1/2 cups pear juice

1/2 cup sugar

1 1/2 cups cold tonic water

1/2 cup cold vodka

1 cup peeled and pitted fresh lychees or drained canned lychees

IN A BOWL, sprinkle the gelatin evenly over the cold water and allow the gelatin to absorb the water for 2 minutes.

Meanwhile, in a saucepan, bring the pear juice and sugar just to a boil over medium heat, stirring to dissolve the sugar. Remove from the heat. Add the gelatin mixture and stir until it is fully dissolved. Let the mixture cool; stir in the tonic and vodka. Refrigerate until thickened (see page 9). Fold in the lychees. Spoon into a 5-cup mold or 6 to 10 martini glasses. Refrigerate until firm (see page 9). Unmold and serve, or serve in the martini glasses.

raspberry cosmo

The sophistication of a cosmopolitan with the sweet, fruity taste of raspberry. Perfect for anyone who values the immense health benefits of berries, as well as people like myself, who value the immense health benefits of vodka.

2 tablespoons (2 envelopes) unflavored gelatin powder

1/2 cup cold water

1¼ cups cranberry juice

1/2 cup sugar

3/4 cup cold triple sec

1/2 cup cold vodka

2 tablespoons lime juice

1 cup fresh raspberries

IN A LARGE BOWL, sprinkle the gelatin evenly over the cold water and allow the gelatin to absorb the water for 2 minutes. In a saucepan, bring the cranberry juice and sugar just to a boil over medium heat. Remove from the heat. Pour the boiling mixture into the gelatin and stir until the gelatin is fully dissolved. Let the mixture cool; stir in the triple sec, vodka, and lime juice. Refrigerate until thickened (see page 9). Fold in the raspberries. Spoon into a 4-cup mold or 5 to 8 martini glasses. Refrigerate until firm (see page 9). Unmold and serve, or serve in the martini glasses.

coffee kahlúa

Makes one 4-cup gelatin mold or 5 to 8 individual molds

Rather than offering guests subpar coffee in twelve-year-old "World's Best Teacher" mugs, consider this ingenious and classy Kahlúa Jell-O. Dinner guests will get their coffee fix in a sculpted, personal mold topped with whipped cream and chocolate shavings. If you want to go all out, serve them in in chocolate dessert cups of you own making (see Chocolate Raspberry Mousse Cups, page 39).

2 tablespoons (2 envelopes) unflavored gelatin powder

1/2 cup cold water

1 1/2 cups boiling strong coffee

1 1/4 cups (14-ounce can) sweetened condensed milk

1/2 cup Kahlúa

Whipped cream, for garnish

Dark chocolate shavings, for garnish

IN A BOWL, sprinkle the gelatin evenly over the cold water and allow the gelatin to absorb the water for 2 minutes. Pour the boiling coffee into the gelatin and stir until the gelatin is fully dissolved. Add the sweetened condensed milk and Kahlúa and stir until the mixture is smooth. Let the mixture cool to room temperature. Pour into a 4-cup mold or 5 to 8 individual molds or serving cups. Refrigerate until firm (see page 9).

To serve, unmold or leave in the serving cups and top with whipped cream and shaved chocolate.

mudslide

Much smoother than the natural disaster of the same name, my Mudslide mixes cream with both coffee and Irish cream liqueur: a velvety refined mold for the gelatin connoisseur. Try this Jell-O while relaxing in the leather club chair in your extensive wood-paneled private library, assuming you have one of those.

2 tablespoons (2 envelopes) unflavored gelatin powder

1/2 cup cold water

3/4 cup boiling water

3/4 cup coffee liqueur

3/4 cup Irish cream liqueur

1/2 cup heavy cream

1/4 cup cold vodka

IN A BOWL, sprinkle the gelatin evenly over the cold water and allow the gelatin to absorb the water for 2 minutes. Add the boiling water and stir until the gelatin is fully dissolved. Whisk in the coffee liqueur, Irish cream liqueur, cream, and vodka until smooth. Spoon into a 4-cup mold or 4 to 7 individual molds. Refrigerate until firm (see page 9). Unmold and serve.

FRUIT-AND-CREAM
LAYERED MOLDS

PEOPLE ARE SO COMPLEX, how can you expect their Jell-Os to be simple? Layering Jell-Os is both visually beautiful and delicious, melding flavors while keeping them distinct. Pair translucent layers with opaque, fruity layers with creamy, sweet with tart. Every gelatin yin has its gelatin yang, and layering is the perfect way to bring them together. Start with a bunny slope of a Jell-O and end by making the Classic Rainbow Mold—the black diamond of all gelatins. Creating layers can be tricky, so be sure to refer to the table on page 9 when creating these recipes to ensure successful results.

peaches and cream

Makes one 9-cup gelatin mold

Sweet, velvety peaches and cream—a summer indulgence as welcome as that five-hundred-dollar vacation-resort package, but sweeter, more sensuous, and with fewer screaming three-year-olds. For a nonalcoholic version, substitute cold water for the peach schnapps.

First Layer

2 cups boiling water

2 (3-ounce) packages peach-flavored gelatin

3/4 cup cold water

3/4 cup cold peach schnapps

2 cups peeled, pitted, and sliced fresh peaches or well-drained canned sliced peaches

Second Layer

2 tablespoons (2 envelopes) unflavored gelatin powder

1/2 cup cold water

1 1/2 cups boiling water

1 1/4 cups (14-ounce can) sweetened condensed milk

TO MAKE THE FIRST LAYER, in a bowl, add the boiling water to the gelatin and stir until the gelatin is fully dissolved. Stir in the cold water and peach schnapps. Refrigerate until thickened (see page 9).

Arrange some of the peach slices in the bottom of a 9-cup mold. Reserve the remaining peaches. Spoon the thickened peach gelatin into the mold over the arranged peach slices. Refrigerate until gelatin is set but not firm (see page 9).

Meanwhile, to make the second layer, in a separate bowl, sprinkle the gelatin over the cold water and allow the gelatin to absorb the water for 2 minutes. Add the boiling water and stir until the gelatin is fully dissolved. Pour in the sweetened condensed milk and stir until the mixture is smooth.

CONTINUED

Refrigerate the mixture until slightly thickened (see page 9). Chop up any remaining peach slices and fold into the milk mixture. Gently spoon into the mold over the peach gelatin layer. Refrigerate until firm (see page 9). Unmold and serve.

blueberry yogurt

This gelatin layers a cascade of fresh blueberries with sweet yogurt. It's one of those rare things that is both enjoyable and good for you. Sort of like a really exciting documentary but more jiggly. This recipe also makes a good parfait treat when served in pint glasses.

First Layer

1 cup boiling water

1 (3-ounce) package blueberry-flavored gelatin

3/4 cup cold water

1 cup fresh blueberries

Second Layer

2 cups boiling water

2 (3-ounce) packages blueberry-flavored gelatin

2 cups vanilla yogurt

TO MAKE THE FIRST LAYER, in a bowl, add the boiling water to the gelatin and stir until the gelatin is fully dissolved. Stir in the cold water. Refrigerate the mixture until thickened (see page 9). Fold the blueberries into the gelatin and spoon into a 7-cup mold or 4 pint glasses. Refrigerate until the gelatin is set but not firm (see page 9).

Meanwhile, to make the second layer, in another bowl, pour the boiling water into the gelatin and stir until the gelatin is fully dissolved. Whisk in the yogurt until the mixture is smooth. Let the mixture cool to room temperature, then gently spoon into the mold over the blueberry gelatin layer. Refrigerate until firm (see page 9). Unmold and serve, or serve in the pint glasses.

cherry cream

Makes one 5-cup gelatin mold

Upbeat and comforting, cherries and cream is the sort of nostalgic flavor combination perfect for getting you through those winter doldrums, that rough breakup, that skateboarding accident, or that horrific haircut. For whatever ails you, it's delicious. If you want to add a little intoxicating fun, try substituting a bit of vodka (up to $1/2$ cup) for some of the water in the first layer.

First Layer

1 cup boiling water

1 (3-ounce) package cherry-flavored gelatin

$3/4$ cup cold water

Second Layer

1 tablespoon (1 envelope) unflavored gelatin powder

$1/4$ cup cold water

$13/4$ cups boiling water

1 (3-ounce) package cherry-flavored gelatin

$11/4$ cups (14-ounce can) sweetened condensed milk

TO MAKE THE FIRST LAYER, in a bowl, add the boiling water to the cherry gelatin and stir until the gelatin is fully dissolved. Stir in the cold water. Let the mixture cool to room temperature, then pour into a 5-cup mold. Refrigerate until the gelatin is set but not firm (see page 9).

Meanwhile, to make the second layer, in a separate bowl, sprinkle the unflavored gelatin over the cold water and allow the gelatin to absorb the water for 2 minutes. Add the boiling water and stir until the gelatin is fully dissolved. Add the cherry gelatin and stir until fully dissolved. Add the sweetened condensed milk and stir until the mixture is smooth. Let the mixture cool to room temperature, then gently spoon into the mold over the cherry gelatin layer. Refrigerate until firm (see page 9). Unmold and serve.

orange chocolate

Makes one 6-cup gelatin mold

I'm not sure who first decided to combine the flavors of orange and choco-late. Perhaps it occurred during the marriage of a bonbon-loving housewife to a scurvy-wary pirate, or the union of a longtime Florida citrus farmer with a Milton Hershey–type entrepreneur. Regardless, the tang of fresh oranges mixed with smooth, sweet chocolate quickly took the candy shelves by storm. Enjoy them both immersed in Jell-O in this scrumptious dessert.

First Layer

1 tablespoon (1 envelope) unflavored gelatin powder

1/4 cup cold water

1 cup boiling water

1/4 cup sugar

1 teaspoon orange extract

1/2 cup mandarin orange slices, fresh or canned and drained

TO MAKE THE FIRST LAYER, in a bowl, sprinkle the gela-tin over the cold water and allow the gelatin to absorb the water for 2 minutes. Add the boiling water and stir until the gelatin is fully dissolved. Add the sugar and orange extract and stir until the sugar is dissolved. Refrigerate the mixture until thickened (see page 9). Arrange the mandarin orange slices on the bottom of a 6-cup mold and gently spoon the clear gelatin into the mold over the orange slices. Refriger-ate until the gelatin is set but not firm (see page 9).

Meanwhile, to make the second layer, in a large saucepan, whisk together the milk, cocoa, sugar, orange extract, and orange zest. Bring just to a boil over medium heat, being careful not to let the milk mixture boil over. Remove from the heat.

Second Layer

3 cups milk

3/4 cup natural unsweetened cocoa powder

1 cup sugar

1 tablespoon orange extract

1 tablespoon freshly grated orange zest

2 tablespoons (2 envelopes) unflavored gelatin powder

1/2 cup cold water

In a separate bowl, sprinkle the gelatin evenly over the cold water and allow the gelatin to absorb the water for 2 minutes. Add the hot milk mixture and stir until the gelatin is fully dissolved. Let the mixture cool to room temperature, then gently spoon into the mold over the mandarin orange layer. Refrigerate until firm (see page 9). Unmold and serve.

minty watermelon ice cream

Makes one 6-cup gelatin mold

The refreshing tastes of mint and watermelon are delicious. Ice cream is delicious. Summer is delicious. The only challenge remaining is to make minty watermelon-scented air come out of my air conditioner. I'm working on it. Note: The more you like the flavor of mint, the longer you can simmer the mint in this recipe. This ice cream treat is best served cold immediately after unmolding and prefers not to be left out in the sun for too long.

First Layer

1 cup fresh mint leaves

3/4 cup sugar

13/4 cups cold water

1 tablespoon (1 envelope) unflavored gelatin powder

1 cup diced, seeded watermelon

Second Layer

2 tablespoons (2 envelopes) unflavored gelatin powder

1/2 cup cold water

1 cup boiling water

1/4 cup sugar

2 cups (1 pint) vanilla ice cream, at room temperature

TO MAKE THE FIRST LAYER, in a saucepan, bring the mint leaves, sugar, and 1½ cups of the water to a boil over high heat. Decrease the heat to low and simmer for 5 minutes, stirring occasionally. Strain out the mint leaves.

In a bowl, sprinkle the gelatin evenly over the remaining 1/4 cup water and allow the gelatin to absorb the water for 2 minutes. Add the boiling mint-infused water and stir until the gelatin is fully dissolved. Refrigerate until thickened (see page 9). Fold in the watermelon and spoon into a 6-cup mold. Refrigerate until the gelatin is set but not firm (see page 9).

Meanwhile, to make the second layer, in a separate bowl, sprinkle the gelatin over the cold water and allow the gelatin to absorb the water for 2 minutes. Add the boiling water and stir until the gelatin is fully dissolved. Add the sugar and stir until dissolved. Add the ice cream and stir until the mixture is smooth. Let the mixture cool to room temperature, then gently spoon into the mold over the minty watermelon gelatin layer. Refrigerate until firm (see page 9). Unmold and serve.

classic rainbow mold

Makes one 7-cup gelatin mold

The way I see it, if you want the rainbow, you gotta put up with the rain.
–DOLLY PARTON

No quote embodies more clearly the experience of creating the ten-layer rainbow mold. The quintessential classic Jell-O recipe, the rainbow mold pops up in nearly every gelatin cookbook. My version uses sweetened condensed milk rather than sour cream or yogurt because it tastes better and dissolves more smoothly. The rainbow mold is visually stunning, but requires so much patience that it would cause Tibetan monks to tear out their hair—if they had any. Undertaking it is no easy feat, but if you succeed, the end result is undeniably beautiful. Note: Timing is key with this mold, so get organized before you begin. I've also included time estimates for each stage to help keep you on track.

6¼ cups boiling water

5 (3-ounce) packages flavored gelatin in 5 different colors

1¼ cups (14-ounce can) sweetened condensed milk

IN A SMALL BOWL, add 1¼ cups of the boiling water to 1 package of the gelatin and stir until the gelatin is fully dissolved. Let the mixture cool to room temperature, then pour ¾ cup of the dissolved gelatin mixture into a 7-cup mold. Refrigerate until set but not firm (about 15 minutes). Add 3 tablespoons of the sweetened condensed milk to the remaining gelatin and stir until the mixture is smooth. Let the mixture cool to room temperature, then pour over the

CONTINUED

clear gelatin layer in the mold. Refrigerate until set but not firm (about 15 minutes).

Repeat the process for each flavor to create 10 layers, 1 clear and 1 opaque layer of all 5 Jell-O colors. Remember that the gelatin must cool to room temperature or cooler before spooning it over the layer already in the mold. It may be best to use 2 small bowls for each flavor, one for the clear and one for the opaque gelatin to cool in before pouring each into the mold. Have 2 additional small bowls on hand so you can begin to prepare the next flavor layers while the preceding layer is cooling.

Refrigerate the finished mold until firm (see page 9). Unmold and serve.

banana cream pie

Makes one 8-cup gelatin mold (or one 10-cup mold if crust layer is doubled)

The banana cream pie, popular for hitting clowns in the face, makes a stunning comeback in this sumptuous Jell-O creation. It can be eaten or thrown at passersby, depending on one's mood. As with all the multilayered molds, timing is key. This recipe is a little tricky, so be sure to pay close attention to each layer's consistency as you go. Due to the timing of the layers, this recipe calls for the second layer to be prepared before the first. Also, depending on the circumference of the mold, it may be necessary to double the recipe for the crust layer to cover the banana layer completely. Note: Banana nectar comes bottled and can be obtained at some grocery stores or most natural foods stores.

Banana Cream Layers

3 tablespoons (3 envelopes) unflavored gelatin powder

3/4 cup cold water

1 1/4 cups boiling water

1/2 cup sugar

2 cups banana nectar

1 cup sweetened condensed milk

1/2 cup chopped banana

1 cup banana slices

TO MAKE THE BANANA CREAM LAYERS, in a bowl, sprinkle 2 tablespoons of the gelatin evenly over 1/2 cup of the cold water and allow the gelatin to absorb the water for 2 minutes. Add 1 cup of the boiling water and stir until the gelatin is fully dissolved. Add the sugar and banana nectar and stir until the sugar is dissolved. Refrigerate until thickened (see page 9), or place in the freezer to speed up thickening.

Meanwhile, in a separate bowl, sprinkle the remaining 1 tablespoon gelatin evenly over the remaining 1/4 cup cold water and allow the gelatin to absorb the water for

CONTINUED

banana cream pie,
continued

Crust Layer

1 tablespoon (1 envelope)
unflavored gelatin powder

3/4 cup milk

1½ cups crushed vanilla wafers

2 minutes. Add the remaining 1/4 cup boiling water and stir until the gelatin is fully dissolved. Add the sweetened condensed milk and stir until the mixture is smooth. Leave out at room temperature until thickened (see page 9).

Once the sweetened condensed milk layer is thickened, stir in the chopped bananas. Spoon into an 8-cup mold. Refrigerate until the gelatin is set but not firm (see page 9). (Check on the consistency of the banana nectar layer and wait for it to be nearly thickened before refrigerating this layer.)

Once the sweetened condensed milk layer is set but not firm and the banana nectar layer is thickened, gently spoon some of the banana nectar gelatin over the sweetened condensed milk layer in the mold. Arrange the banana slices on the banana nectar gelatin in the mold, spacing them 1/2 inch apart. Spoon the remaining banana nectar gelatin into the mold over the banana slices. Refrigerate until the gelatin is set but not firm (see page 9).

To make the crust layer, in a saucepan, sprinkle the gelatin evenly over the milk and allow the gelatin to absorb the milk for 2 minutes. Bring the milk just to a boil over medium heat, being careful not to let the milk boil over. Remove from the heat. Let the mixture cool to room temperature, then stir in the vanilla wafer crumbs. Gently spoon into the mold over the banana gelatin layer. Refrigerate until firm (see page 9). Unmold and serve.

SEASONAL HOLIDAY MOLDS

MAKE SURE YOU THOUGHTFULLY MATCH THE GELATIN to the celebration, or you'll be serving a red-white-and blue Jell-O at Thanksgiving, eggnog on the Fourth of July, and "brains" at your sister's baby shower. But properly organized, these gelatins are much more welcome than fruitcake, dry turkey, or those multigallon Christmas popcorn tins that everyone's received but no one in history has ever wanted (except, bizarrely, my cousin).

berry fourth of july

Makes one 6-cup gelatin mold

For those who love strawberries, blueberries, vanilla ice cream, and patriotism, this Jell-O will make you wish you could hit all the notes in "The Star-Spangled Banner." Now is the time to use that star-shaped mold. Note: This ice cream treat is best served cold immediately after unmolding.

First Layer

1 tablespoon (1 envelope) unflavored gelatin powder

1/4 cup cold water

1 cup boiling water

1/2 cup sugar

1/2 cup fresh blueberries

1/2 cup sliced fresh strawberries

Second Layer

2 tablespoons (2 envelopes) unflavored gelatin powder

1/2 cup cold water

1 cup boiling water

1/4 cup sugar

2 cups (1 pint) vanilla ice cream, at room temperature

TO MAKE THE FIRST LAYER, in a bowl, sprinkle the gelatin over the cold water and allow the gelatin to absorb the water for 2 minutes. Add the boiling water and stir until the gelatin is fully dissolved. Stir in the sugar. Refrigerate until thickened (see page 9). Arrange the blueberries and strawberries in a pattern on the bottom of a 6-cup mold, then gently spoon the clear gelatin over the top. Refrigerate until the gelatin is set but not firm (see page 9).

Meanwhile, to make the second layer, in a separate bowl, sprinkle the gelatin over the cold water and allow the gelatin to absorb the water for 2 minutes. Add the boiling water and stir until the gelatin is fully dissolved. Add the sugar and stir until dissolved. Stir in the ice cream until the mixture is smooth. Let the mixture cool to room temperature, then spoon into the mold over the berry layer. Refrigerate until firm (see page 9). Unmold and serve.

brains!!!

Are you:

A. Looking for the perfect food for a Halloween get-together?
B. A licensed neurologist with a wonderful sense of humor?
C. Hoping to bond with your seven-year-old son?
D. Uncertain of what to serve during the zombie uprising?

If the answer to any of these questions is yes, then grab your brain-shaped mold and make the recipe listed below. Note: Substitute fruit juice, such as orange or apple, for the vodka if you wish to serve this to children.

1½ cups boiling water

2 (3-ounce) packages strawberry-flavored gelatin

1½ cups whipped cream (about ¾ cup heavy cream, whipped)

1 cup vodka

1 cup chopped fresh or frozen and thawed strawberries

IN A BOWL, add the boiling water to the gelatin and stir until gelatin is fully dissolved. Add the whipped cream and whisk until smooth. Stir in the vodka. Refrigerate until thickened (see page 9). Stir to mix in any whipped cream skin that has risen to the top. Fold in the strawberries and spoon into a 5-cup mold. Refrigerate until firm (see page 9). Unmold and serve.

pumpkin pie

Makes one 4-cup gelatin mold or 5 to 8 individual molds

So okay, there wasn't any pumpkin pie Jell-O at the first Thanksgiving, but you know what else wasn't at the first Thanksgiving? Your uncle's weird girlfriend. Or thirty of your relatives burping and loosening their pants in a vain attempt to make room for dessert. Here's something new that will become a *welcome* tradition. A blend of creamy pumpkin with nutmeg and cinnamon, the pumpkin pie Jell-O will give the family something positive to talk about . . . for a change. Note: This recipe can be poured into a fun pumpkin-shaped mold or served as mini-pies in tart-size pie crusts.

2 cups (15-ounce can) canned pumpkin

1/4 cup granulated sugar

1/2 cup firmly packed dark brown sugar

1 teaspoon ground cinnamon

1/4 teaspoon ground nutmeg

2 tablespoons (2 envelopes) unflavored gelatin powder

1/2 cup cold water

3/4 cup boiling water

1 cup sweetened condensed milk

IN A BOWL, fold together the pumpkin, granulated sugar, brown sugar, cinnamon, and nutmeg, mixing until smooth.

In a separate bowl, sprinkle the gelatin evenly over the cold water and allow the gelatin to absorb the water for 2 minutes. Add the boiling water and stir until the gelatin is fully dissolved. Add the sweetened condensed milk and stir until the mixture is smooth.

Add the gelatin mixture to the pumpkin mixture and beat with an electric mixer until smooth. Spoon into a 4-cup mold or 5 to 8 individual molds. Refrigerate until firm (see page 9). Unmold and serve.

eggnog rum

Makes one 6-cup gelatin mold

Smooth, dark rum mixed with rich, creamy eggnog is a wonderful way to enjoy/tolerate/survive the holidays. It's not written in stone that you have to leave *cookies* for Santa. Note: If you plan on serving this to the elderly, pregnant, young, or infirm, be sure to use pasteurized eggnog or eggnog that doesn't contain raw eggs.

3 tablespoons (3 envelopes) unflavored gelatin powder

2 cups cold water

2³/4 cups eggnog

3/4 cup sweetened condensed milk

1/2 cup dark rum

1 teaspoon ground nutmeg

IN A SAUCEPAN, sprinkle the gelatin evenly over the cold water and allow the gelatin to absorb the water for 2 minutes. Bring just to a boil over medium-high heat, stirring until the gelatin is fully dissolved. Transfer to a bowl, add the eggnog, sweetened condensed milk, rum, and nutmeg, and stir until the mixture is smooth. Pour into a 6-cup mold. Refrigerate until firm (see page 9). Unmold and serve.

hot chile chocolate

Makes one 4-cup gelatin mold or 5 to 8 individual molds

Although aspects of the Aztec culture aren't commonly used in today's world (the Aztec calendar is not easily converted to the quirky "page-a-day" format), some of the traditions hang in there, and the penchant for adding hot chiles to chocolate seems like it might stick around for a while. This recipe brings that flavor combination into the twenty-first century, with modern conveniences like chili powder and cocoa powder—no trip to the rain forest required. Note: Add less chili powder if you can't handle the spice and more if you like having the inside of your mouth to feel like a volcano going through menopause.

3 cups whole or 2 percent milk

1/2 cup natural unsweetened cocoa powder

1 cup sugar

2 teaspoons vanilla extract

1 teaspoon ground cinnamon

1 or 2 teaspoons chili powder (depending how hot you like it)

2 tablespoons (2 envelopes) unflavored gelatin powder

1/2 cup cold water

IN A SAUCEPAN, whisk together the milk, cocoa, sugar, vanilla, cinnamon and chili powder. Bring just to a boil over medium heat, being careful not to let the milk mixture boil over. Remove from the heat.

In a bowl, sprinkle the gelatin evenly over the cold water and allow the gelatin to absorb the water for 2 minutes. Add the boiled milk mixture to the gelatin mixture and stir until fully dissolved. Let the mixture cool to room temperature, then gently spoon into a 4-cup mold or 5 to 8 individual molds. Refrigerate until firm (see page 9). Unmold and serve.

gingerbread men

Makes 6 cups, or about 10 gingerbread men

While constructing a gingerbread house out of gelatin might be structurally challenging, there's no reason you can't enjoy a lively population of gingerbread men (and women). Decorate them with sprinkles, nuts, and chocolate chips.

4 tablespoons (4 envelopes) unflavored gelatin powder

1 cup cold water

2 cups boiling water

2 1/2 cups (two 14-ounce cans) sweetened condensed milk

1/4 cup molasses

2 teaspoons ground ginger

2 teaspoons ground cinnamon

1/2 teaspoon ground nutmeg

2 teaspoons vanilla extract

Sprinkles, chocolate chips, and/or slivered almonds, for decorating

IN A LARGE BOWL, sprinkle the gelatin evenly over the cold water and allow the gelatin to absorb the water for 2 minutes. Add the boiling water to the gelatin mixture and stir until fully dissolved. Add the sweetened condensed milk, molasses, ginger, cinnamon, nutmeg, and vanilla and stir until the mixture is smooth. Refrigerate until it begins to thicken (see page 9). Spoon onto a rimmed baking sheet. Refrigerate until firm (see page 9).

Dip the bottom of the baking sheet in warm water for 15 seconds to loosen the gelatin. Use gingerbread-man cookie cutters to cut the gelatin into shapes and gently lift from the pan with a spatula. Decorate and serve.

spiced wassail

Makes one 7-cup gelatin mold

Wassailing is an ancient tradition from southern England that involves singing to trees in apple orchards to ensure a good crop of cider apples for the next year's harvest. So before you spend an hour kneeling in front of fruit trees, belting out whatever Beyoncé song you can remember the words to, try this delightful fall blend of cider, allspice, orange rind, cloves, and cinnamon.

4 cups apple juice or pasteurized apple cider

1 cup cranberry juice

10 whole cloves

10 allspice berries

2 cinnamon sticks

3/4 cup sugar

1/2 orange with rind

4 tablespoons (4 envelopes) unflavored gelatin powder

1 cup cold water

3/4 cup dark rum

2 orange slices each studded with 4 whole cloves, for garnish

IN A SAUCEPAN, bring the apple juice, cranberry juice, cloves, allspice, cinnamon, sugar, and orange to a boil over high heat. Cover, decrease the heat to low, and simmer for at least 45 minutes, stirring occasionally. Strain out the cloves, allspice, and cinnamon sticks; squeeze the liquid out of the orange into the juice mixture and discard the fruit.

Meanwhile, in a bowl, sprinkle the gelatin over the cold water and allow the gelatin to absorb the water for 2 minutes. Add the juice mixture and stir until the gelatin is fully dissolved. Stir in the rum. Refrigerate until thickened (see page 9). Spoon into a 7-cup mold. Refrigerate until firm (see page 9). Unmold, garnish with the orange slices, and serve.

AMERICANA AND
OTHER FAVORITES

*H*AVE FUN WITH THIS CHAPTER BEFORE EXPERIMENTING and turning your own favorite flavor combinations into a Jell-O. Peanut butter and jelly? Done. Vanilla ice cream and root beer? Accomplished. Those ridiculously addictive Girl Scout Samoa cookies that you look forward to for months at a time because for whatever reason they don't sell them in stores? Have no fear; I got your Samoas right here, baby. Enjoy the tastes of Americana embodied in that most American of desserts—Jell-O.

petite watermelons

Makes 20 fruit slices

If the response you're looking for when you unveil your gelatin is, "Ohhhhh, it's so *cute*!" this recipe will do it. After seeing these little creations on various foodie blogs around the Web, I was inspired to make my own version of these treats. A sweet strawberry puree encased in a lime rind and sprinkled with tiny black seeds, these tiny watermelon slices will have people fawning over their inherent adorableness (the hard part is getting people to stop gushing and eat them). Note: This recipe is best served within a day of preparation, as the lime rinds will make the gelatin bitter if stored for too long.

1 cup boiling water

1 (3-ounce) package strawberry-flavored gelatin

1 cup chopped fresh or frozen and thawed strawberries

1/2 cup cold water or vodka

5 limes, halved, pulp scooped out and discarded, and rind halves reserved

1 teaspoon black sesame seeds, poppy seeds, or basil seeds

IN A BOWL, add the boiling water to the gelatin and stir until the gelatin is fully dissolved. Transfer the gelatin to a blender. Add the strawberries and cold water and blend until liquefied. Refrigerate until thickened (see page 9). Skim off any foam that has risen to the top of the gelatin mixture and stir to evenly distribute the strawberry puree. Spoon into the lime rind halves. Refrigerate until firm (see page 9).

Carefully halve the gelatin-filled lime rinds again. Sprinkle with the seeds and serve.

tiramisu

Makes 8 cups gelatin

This sweet Italian dessert makes me want to cry *"Mangia!"* because it's delicious, and I really don't know any other relevant words in Italian. In several delightful layers and served in squares rather than unmolded, this tiramisu incorporates the flavors of coffee-soaked ladyfingers, vanilla, and mascarpone cheese sweetened with condensed milk, all held neatly together with a bit of gelatin. To make this treat even fancier, try using coffee-flavored liqueur in place of the coffee.

2 tablespoons (2 envelopes) unflavored gelatin powder

2 cups cold water

2 cups (16 ounces) mascarpone cheese

1 cup sweetened condensed milk

4 teaspoons vanilla extract

16 ladyfingers

1 cup strong coffee

1 tablespoon natural unsweetened cocoa powder

IN A SMALL SAUCEPAN, sprinkle the gelatin evenly over the cold water and allow the gelatin to absorb the water for 2 minutes. Bring just to a boil over medium-high heat, stirring until the gelatin is fully dissolved. Transfer to a bowl, add the mascarpone cheese, sweetened condensed milk, and vanilla, and beat with an electric mixer until the mixture is smooth. Refrigerate until slightly thickened (see page 9).

Meanwhile, lightly coat the ladyfingers with the coffee (I find it easiest to pour the coffee into a saucer and dip both sides of each ladyfinger into it). Arrange half of the ladyfingers evenly in the bottom of a 2-quart baking dish or equivalent-size container.

Gently spoon half of the gelatin-mascarpone mixture evenly over the ladyfingers, covering them completely. Refrigerate until the gelatin is set but not firm (see page 9). Leave the remaining gelatin mixture at room temperature. Once the chilled gelatin mixture is set, arrange the remaining ladyfingers over the first layer and gently spoon the remaining gelatin mixture evenly over the top. Refrigerate until firm (see page 9).

Sprinkle the cocoa powder over the top and slice into squares (instead of unmolding) to serve.

samoa

Samoas (called Caramel Delights in some parts of the country) are cookies that are so dangerously addictive that they encourage us to form a junkie-dealer type of relationship with our local Girl Scouts. But before you find yourself donning sunglasses, standing on street corners, and cutting a deal on eight boxes with someone named "Ashley," try this Samoa gelatin. Rich and buttery with toasted coconut and drizzled with chocolate, it's a delightful treat that can be obtained without a sash-sporting, patch-collecting, beanie-wearing middleman. Note: To toast your own coconut flakes, spread the flaked coconut on a baking sheet and bake in a preheated 350˚F oven, stirring occasionally, for about 8 minutes, until golden, being careful not to let the coconut burn. You can do this before you start the recipe, as the coconut does not need to be warm when you add it to the gelatin mixture.

1/2 cup sugar

1/2 cup light corn syrup

1 tablespoon butter

1 cup milk

2 tablespoons (2 envelopes) unflavored gelatin powder

3/4 cup cold water

1 teaspoon vanilla extract

1/2 cup sweetened condensed milk

IN A SAUCEPAN, stir together the sugar, corn syrup, butter, and milk and bring just to a boil over medium heat. Remove from the heat.

Meanwhile, in a large bowl, sprinkle the gelatin evenly over the cold water and allow the gelatin to absorb the water for 2 minutes. Add the milk mixture and stir until the gelatin is fully dissolved. Stir in the vanilla and sweetened condensed milk. Refrigerate until thickened (see page 9). Fold in the toasted coconut and spoon into a 5-cup mold. Refrigerate until firm (see page 9).

2 cups toasted coconut flakes (see headnote)

1/2 cup semisweet chocolate chips

1 tablespoon solid vegetable shortening

Unmold the gelatin. In a small saucepan, heat the chocolate chips and shortening over high heat, stirring continuously until melted. Drizzle over the mold in stripes. Refrigerate for about 30 minutes, until the chocolate has hardened.

root beer float squares

Makes 7 cups gelatin

Break out your poodle skirt, your bobby socks, and your recording of "Tutti Frutti" by Little Richard. A Jell-O reprising a classic soda-fountain combo of root beer with smooth vanilla ice cream is the perfect way to relive the sweet black-and-white decade that was the 1950s. Plop this gelatin on a red-and-white-checkered tablecloth while you lie whimsically in the family room, watching reruns of *Father Knows Best*. Note: This recipe requires you to prepare the root beer layer 3 to 6 hours before the ice cream layer.

4 tablespoons (4 envelopes) unflavored gelatin powder

1 cup cold water

1 1/2 cups boiling water

3/4 cup sugar

2 cups root beer

2 cups (1 pint) vanilla ice cream

IN A BOWL, sprinkle 2 tablespoons of the gelatin over 1/2 cup of the cold water and allow the gelatin to absorb the water for 2 minutes. Add 1/2 cup of the boiling water and stir until the gelatin is fully dissolved. Stir in 1/2 cup of the sugar and the root beer until the sugar is dissolved. Skim off any foam created by the root beer. Pour into a 2-quart baking dish and refrigerate until firm (3 hours, or overnight for best results).

Once firm, cut the root beer gelatin into 1/2-inch cubes in the baking dish. With a spatula, carefully loosen the cubes from the dish and mix them around so they are haphazardly arranged in the dish. Refrigerate the root beer cubes while you prepare the next step.

CONTINUED

root beer float squares,
continued

In a large bowl, sprinkle the remaining 2 tablespoons gelatin over the remaining 1/2 cup cold water and allow the gelatin to absorb the water for 2 minutes. Add the remaining 1 cup boiling water and stir until the gelatin is fully dissolved. Add the remaining 1/4 cup sugar and stir until the sugar is dissolved. In a saucepan, melt the ice cream over high heat until it is a liquid. Add the melted ice cream to the gelatin and stir until the mixture is smooth. Let the mixture cool to room temperature, then gently spoon over the root beer cubes in the baking dish. Refrigerate until firm (see page 9). Cut into blocks and serve.

new york cheesecake

Makes one 3-cup gelatin mold or 4 tarts

If there's one thing that embodies the spirit of New York, it's some guy crossing the street, whacking his hand onto the hood of a taxi, and shouting, "I'm WALK-ING here!" But if there were two things, the other would be cheesecake. Or, okay, maybe bagels. But bagels don't make any sense floating inside a Jell-O mold, so let's just go with cheesecake. Note: This recipe has all the flavor of cheesecake and I love to serve it as mini-pies in tart-size crusts, but you can also pour it into your favorite shaped mold. To flavor it up, add 1 teaspoon lemon, orange, or raspberry extract to the mix, or top with your favorite fruit topping.

2 tablespoons (2 envelopes) unflavored gelatin powder

3/4 cup cold water

1 cup (8-ounce brick) cream cheese, very soft room temperature

1/2 cup sour cream

3/4 cup sugar

1 tablespoon vanilla extract

4 (3-inch) baked tart shells (optional)

IN A SMALL SAUCEPAN, sprinkle the gelatin evenly over the cold water and allow the gelatin to absorb the water for 2 minutes. Bring just to a boil over medium-high heat, stirring until the gelatin is fully dissolved. Transfer to a bowl, add the cream cheese, sour cream, sugar, and vanilla, and beat with an electric mixer until smooth. Let the mixture cool to room temperature and divide among the tart shells or spoon into a 3-cup mold. Refrigerate until firm (see page 9). Unmold and serve, or serve in the tart shells.

chocolate peanut butter cups

Makes 6 to 10 cups

For those of you with a sweet tooth, a peanut butter–loving tooth, or an unbridled passion for anything made with chocolate, this is the Jell-O equivalent of a candy bar. Share with guests or frantically eat the entire batch yourself due to a momentary loss of willpower—the Jell-O won't tell.

2¹/₂ cups whole or 2 percent milk

¹/₃ cup natural unsweetened cocoa powder

1 cup sugar

1³/₄ cups peanut butter chips

2 tablespoons (2 envelopes) unflavored gelatin powder

¹/₂ cup cold water

1 teaspoon vanilla extract

IN A SAUCEPAN, whisk together the milk, cocoa, and sugar and bring just to a boil over medium-high heat. Decrease the heat to medium, add the peanut butter chips, and whisk until the chips are melted and the mixture is smooth.

In a bowl, sprinkle the gelatin evenly over the cold water and allow the gelatin to absorb the water for 2 minutes. Add the hot milk mixture and whisk until the gelatin is fully dissolved. Stir in the vanilla.

Refrigerate until thickened (see page 9). Spoon into 6 to 10 foil baking cups or individual molds. Refrigerate until firm (see page 9). Unmold (if using baking cups, it might be helpful to dip them in warm water for just a moment before peeling away the foil) and serve.

peanut butter **and jelly**

Makes 8 cups gelatin

This Jell-O so reminiscent of school lunches that it should be served inside a brown bag with an apple and a juice box. It combines grape gelatin with either creamy or chunky peanut butter and a graham cracker crust. Best when eaten at long communal tables with lunch ladies telling everybody to quiet down.

Peanut Butter and Jelly Layers

1³/₄ cups boiling water

1 (3-ounce) package grape-flavored gelatin

1 cup cold water

1 tablespoon (1 envelope) unflavored gelatin powder

¹/₂ cup sugar

³/₄ cup peanut butter (creamy or chunky)

TO MAKE THE JELLY LAYER, in a bowl, add 1 cup of the boiling water to the grape gelatin and stir until the gelatin is fully dissolved. Stir in ³/₄ cup of the cold water. Spoon the gelatin into a 2-quart baking dish. Refrigerate until set but not firm (see page 9).

Meanwhile, to make the peanut butter layer, in a separate bowl, sprinkle the unflavored gelatin over the remaining ¹/₄ cup cold water and allow the gelatin to absorb the water for 2 minutes. Add the remaining ³/₄ cup boiling water and stir until the gelatin is fully dissolved. Stir in the sugar until dissolved. Whisk in the peanut butter until smooth. Let the mixture cool to room temperature, then gently spoon over the grape layer in the baking dish. Refrigerate until the gelatin is set but not firm (see page 9).

Crust Layer

2 tablespoons (2 envelopes) unflavored gelatin powder

1 1/2 cups milk

2 cups crushed chocolate graham cracker crumbs

To make the crust layer, in a saucepan, sprinkle the unflavored gelatin evenly over the milk and allow the gelatin to absorb the milk for 2 minutes. Bring the milk just to a boil over medium heat, being careful not to let the milk boil over. Remove from the heat. Let the mixture cool to room temperature, then stir in the graham cracker crumbs. Gently spoon into the mold over the peanut butter layer. Refrigerate until firm (see page 9).

Slice into cubes, invert the cubes so the crust side is down, and serve.

strawberry nutella

Makes one 6-cup gelatin mold

In the fine tradition of Europeans putting Nutella on, well, everything, I bring you the Strawberry Nutella mold. Think the smoothness of chocolate-covered strawberries only . . . you know . . . with Nutella. Note: If you don't care for or are allergic to strawberries, bananas or raspberries are a great substitute.

First Layer

1 tablespoons (1 envelope) unflavored gelatin powder

1/4 cup cold water

1 cup boiling water

1/4 cup sugar

1 teaspoon vanilla extract

8 to 10 whole fresh strawberries, tops sliced off and halved

TO MAKE THE FIRST LAYER, in a bowl, sprinkle the gelatin evenly over the cold water and allow the gelatin to absorb the water for 2 minutes. Add the boiling water and stir until the gelatin is fully dissolved. Stir in the sugar and vanilla. Refrigerate until thickened (see page 9). Arrange the strawberry halves in a pattern on the bottom of a 6-cup mold and gently spoon the clear gelatin over the strawberries in the mold. Refrigerate until the gelatin is set but not firm (see page 9). Note: This layer may begin to set faster than the next layer can be prepared, so it may be best to leave it at room temperature until the next layer in nearly ready.

Second Layer

2 tablespoons (2 envelopes) unflavored gelatin powder

1/2 cup cold water

1¹/2 cups boiling water

1¹/2 cups chocolate-hazelnut spread

1/2 cup diced fresh strawberries

Meanwhile, to make the second layer, in a bowl, sprinkle the gelatin evenly over the cold water and allow the gelatin to absorb the water for 2 minutes. Add the boiling water and stir until the gelatin is fully dissolved. Add the chocolate-hazelnut spread and whisk until smooth. Refrigerate the mixture until thickened (see page 9). Fold in the strawberries. Gently spoon into the mold over the clear layer. Refrigerate until firm (see page 9). Unmold and serve.

marshmallow butterscotch

Makes one 6-cup gelatin mold

A child's dream and a dentist's nightmare, this Jell-O wouldn't seem out of place in *Willy Wonka & the Chocolate Factory*. Delicious homemade butterscotch is wrapped around dozens of miniature marshmallows. An ideal indulgence for a winter occasion.

1/2 cup unsalted butter

2 cups firmly packed dark brown sugar

2 1/2 cups milk

2 tablespoons (2 envelopes) unflavored gelatin powder

1/2 cup cold water

1/2 cup boiling water

2 cups miniature marshmallows

IN A SAUCEPAN, melt the butter over medium-low heat, then add the brown sugar, stirring until dissolved. Add the milk and stir, being careful not to bring mixture to a boil.

Meanwhile, in a bowl, sprinkle the gelatin evenly over the cold water and allow the gelatin to absorb the water for 2 minutes. Add the boiling water and stir until the gelatin is fully dissolved. Whisk the milk mixture into the gelatin in the bowl. Refrigerate until thickened (see page 9). Fold in the marshmallows. Spoon into a 6-cup mold. Refrigerate until firm (see page 9). Unmold and serve.

8

VEGAN DELIGHTS

THE WORD *AGAR-AGAR* sounds like something cave people mumbled to each other on wooly mammoth hunts during the Pleistocene epoch. But the substance itself is incredibly helpful in modern times, allowing us to create vegan-friendly gelatins. Agar-agar (which is the Malay word for "jelly") is derived from seaweed, allowing those who have sworn off eating anything with a face to enjoy the recipes in this chapter guilt free. To keep these recipes as healthy and animal friendly as possible, I've replaced cream with soy milk and sugar with maple syrup (other alternative sweeteners like agave nectar and honey can make the gelatin unstable). Enjoy these agar-agar recipes in the company of a four-legged friend.

THINGS TO KNOW ABOUT AGAR-AGAR

YOU WON'T COME ACROSS AGAR-AGAR while browsing the chewing gum aisle in a 7-Eleven. But it can be found at health foods stores, Asian grocery stores, or good-quality supermarkets. If all else fails, it's easily available on the Internet.

The biggest difference between gelatin and agar-agar is the temperature-setting point: agar-agar will set without being chilled too drastically. In other words, gelatin needs to be thrown into the fridge, but agar-agar could technically set at room temperature.

Unmold agar-agar molds the same way as gelatin molds, but because agar-agar gels more firmly and melts at a much higher temperature, dip molds in hot (not warm) water for up to 2 minutes to loosen the agar-agar from the mold. I find it easier to use smaller, individual-size molds that are wider than they are deep.

coconut raspberry agar

Makes 6 cups agar-agar

If you're trapped on a deserted island with the requisite coconut-heavy palm tree, just make sure there are some fresh raspberries in your survival kit and you'll be able to make this fabulous treat while you wait for the search-and-rescue teams. (This assumes the deserted island also has a minifridge and a boiling hot spring.)

4 cups coconut milk

2 cups sugar

9 teaspoons agar-agar powder

3½ cups water

1 teaspoon almond extract

1 cup fresh raspberries

IN A SAUCEPAN, whisk together the coconut milk, 1 cup of the sugar, and 5 teaspoons of the agar-agar powder and bring just to a boil over high heat, being careful not to let the coconut milk boil over. Decrease the heat to medium and whisk continuously for 3 minutes. Pour the mixture into a 2-quart baking dish and refrigerate until set but not firm (about 4 minutes).

Meanwhile, in a separate saucepan, whisk together the water, almond extract, the remaining 1 cup sugar, and the remaining 4 teaspoons agar-agar and bring just to a boil over high heat. Remove from the heat and let the mixture cool to room temperature. Gently spoon the mixture over the coconut layer. As the top layer begins to thicken (this will happen quickly), sink the raspberries down into the

CONTINUED

coconut raspberry agar, *continued*

sugar-water agar, spacing them about 1 inch apart. Refrigerate until firm, about 1 hour. Using a knife or small cookie cutters, cut the agar into blocks or shapes with 1 raspberry in the center of each cutout and gently lift from the dish with an offset spatula. Serve on small plates.

watermelon basil agar

Makes 5 cups agar-agar; 7 to 10 individual molds

Anyone who has planted a spring garden has watched tiny ground-hugging basil plants shoot up like seventeen-year-old boys hitting a growth spurt. This popular herb is used as an accent in everything from mixed drinks to pasta sauces, and the invigorating, pungent smell of fresh basil is the perfect way to punch up the refreshing taste of cold, sweet summer watermelon. Note: If watermelon is not your thing, you can substitute canned pineapple chunks. Don't use fresh or frozen pineapple, however, or the pineapple enzymes may prevent the agar-agar from getting firm.

10 medium fresh basil leaves (about 1/3 cup loosely packed)

2 cups water

3/4 cup sugar

1 tablespoon agar-agar powder

2 cups cubed seeded watermelon

IN A BLENDER or small food processor, process the basil and 1/2 cup of the water until the basil is mostly liquefied.

In a saucepan, bring the remaining 1 1/2 cups water and the sugar to a boil over medium heat. Remove from the heat. Add the agar-agar powder and stir until fully dissolved. Stir in the basil water. Refrigerate until the mixture begins to thicken, 15 to 25 minutes. Stir in the cubed watermelon. Spoon into 7 to 10 individual molds and refrigerate until firm, about 1 hour. Unmold and serve.

rhubarb rosemary agar

Makes 4 cups agar-agar; 5 to 8 individual molds

Rhubarb has been used to battle everything from heartburn to high cholesterol to hot flashes. Combine it with rosemary for a beautifully unique creation that can be served to middle-aged men, menopausal women, or . . . you know . . . anyone.

2 cups chopped rhubarb stems

1/4 cup lemon juice

1 teaspoon dried rosemary

1 cup sugar

2 cups water

4 teaspoons agar-agar powder

IN A SAUCEPAN, bring 1 cup of the rhubarb, lemon juice, rosemary, sugar, and water to a boil over high heat. Decrease the heat to medium-low and simmer for 15 minutes. Strain and discard the solids.

Return the strained rhubarb water to the saucepan and stir in the remaining 1 cup rhubarb. Bring the mixture back to a low boil and stir in the agar-agar powder until fully dissolved. Cook over medium heat for 2 minutes. Remove from the heat. Refrigerate until the mixture begins to thicken, 20 to 30 minutes, then stir to evenly distribute the rhubarb in the mixture. Spoon into 5 to 8 individual molds and refrigerate until firm, about 1 hour. Unmold and serve.

maple soy agar

Throw on your buffalo plaid jacket and settle into your Maine cabin to enjoy this hearty, sweet maple dessert. Enjoy it while whittling something out of a stick.

3 cups vanilla soy milk

4 teaspoons agar-agar powder

1 cup plus 5 to 8 teaspoons pure maple syrup

Chopped pecans or walnuts, for garnish

IN A LARGE SAUCEPAN, bring the soy milk just to a boil over medium heat, being careful not to let it boil over. Remove from the heat. Add the agar-agar powder and stir until fully dissolved. Stir in 1 cup of the maple syrup. Pour into 5 to 8 individual molds and refrigerate until firm, about 1 hour.

Unmold and garnish each mold with 1 teaspoon maple syrup. Sprinkle with chopped nuts and serve.

vanilla clementine panna cotta

Makes 3 cups agar-agar; 4 to 6 individual molds

Is there a more perfect fruit than the clementine, so sweet and seed free and easy to peel? If there are a few left in the crate that you didn't devour immediately after purchasing them, add them to this delightful vegan confection.

1½ cups vanilla soy milk

1 teaspoon agar-agar powder

1½ cups vanilla soy yogurt

2 tablespoons sugar

½ teaspoon freshly grated clementine zest

Clementine slices, for garnish

IN A LARGE SAUCEPAN, bring the soy milk just to a boil over medium heat, being careful not to let the soy milk boil over. Decrease the heat to low and add the agar-agar powder, stirring until fully dissolved. Add the soy yogurt, sugar, and zest and whisk until the mixture is smooth. Pour into 4 to 6 individual molds and refrigerate until firm, about 1 hour.

Unmold, garnish with clementine slices, and serve.

ABOUT THE AUTHOR

Victoria Belanger was born and raised in Roanoke, Virginia. After studying photography at Virginia Commonwealth University, she moved to New York City and began experimenting with creative Jell-O molding and photographing her colorful creations for her website, The Jello Mold Mistress of Brooklyn (jellomoldmistress.com). Victoria and her jiggly masterpieces have been featured in the *New York Times*, *Globe & Mail*, *Food & Wine*, *The Splendid Table*, and *Cute Overload*. In addition to Jell-O molding, she works as a photographer and enjoys exploring the five boroughs of New York City by bicycle.

RAQUEL D'APICE is a freelance writer and comic who lives in Jersey City, New Jersey.

MEASUREMENT CONVERSION CHARTS

Volume

U.S.	Imperial	Metric
1 tablespoon	1/2 fl oz	15 ml
2 tablespoons	1 fl oz	30 ml
1/4 cup	2 fl oz	60 ml
1/3 cup	3 fl oz	90 ml
1/2 cup	4 fl oz	120 ml
2/3 cup	5 fl oz (1/4 pint)	150 ml
3/4 cup	6 fl oz	180 ml
1 cup	8 fl oz (1/3 pint)	240 ml
1 1/4 cups	10 fl oz (1/2 pint)	300 ml
2 cups (1 pint)	16 fl oz (2/3 pint)	480 ml
2 1/2 cups	20 fl oz (1 pint)	600 ml
1 quart	32 fl oz (1 2/3 pint)	1 l

Temperature

Fahrenheit	Celsius/Gas Mark
250°F	120°C/gas mark 1/2
275°F	135°C/gas mark 1
300°F	150°C/gas mark 2
325°F	160°C/gas mark 3
350°F	180 or 175°C/gas mark 4
375°F	190°C/gas mark 5
400°F	200°C/gas mark 6
425°F	220°C/gas mark 7
450°F	230°C/gas mark 8
475°F	245°C/gas mark 9
500°F	260°C

Length

Inch	Metric
1/4 inch	6 mm
1/2 inch	1.25 cm
3/4 inch	2 cm
1 inch	2.5 cm
6 inches (1/2 foot)	15 cm
12 inches (1 foot)	30 cm

Weight

U.S./Imperial	Metric
1/2 oz	15 g
1 oz	30 g
2 oz	60 g
1/4 lb	115 g
1/3 lb	150 g
1/2 lb	225 g
3/4 lb	350 g
1 lb	450 g

INDEX

A

Agar-agar, 105, 106
    Coconut Raspberry Agar, 107–8
    Maple Soy Agar, 113
    Rhubarb Rosemary Agar, 112
    Vanilla Clementine Panna Cotta, 114
    Watermelon Basil Agar, 111
Almonds
    Nuts 'n' Honey, 25
Apples, apple cider, and apple juice
    Spiced Wassail, 86
    White Sangria, 47
Apricot Cream, 39

B

Banana Cream Pie, 73–75
Berries. *See also individual berries*
    Berry Fourth of July, 79
    Pomegranate Berry Salad, 18
Blueberries
    Berry Fourth of July, 79
    Blueberry Yogurt, 63
    Green Milk Tea, 31
Brains!!!, 80
Brandy
    Cheery Cherry Salad, 20
Butterscotch, Marshmallow, 104

C

Carrot Cake, 23–24
Chai Tea Panna Cotta, 41
Champagne
    Mimosa, 46
    Sparkling Champagne and Strawberries, 49
Cheery Cherry Salad, 20
Cheese
    Carrot Cake, 23–24
    New York Cheesecake, 97
    Tiramisu, 90–91
Cherries
    Cheery Cherry Salad, 20
Cherry cola
    Cheery Cherry Salad, 20
Cherry-flavored gelatin
    Cherry Cream, 64
Chile Chocolate, Hot, 83
Chocolate
    Chocolate Peanut Butter Cups, 99
    Chocolate Raspberry Mousse Cups, 37–38
    Grasshopper Pie, 43–44
    Hot Chile Chocolate, 83
    Orange Chocolate, 66–67
    Samoa, 92–93
    Tiramisu, 90–91
Classic Rainbow Mold, 71–72

Clementine Panna Cotta, Vanilla, 114
Coconut
  Samoa, 92–93
  toasting, 92
Coconut milk
  Coconut Raspberry Agar, 107–8
  Piña Colada, 52
Coffee
  Coffee Kahlúa, 56
  Tiramisu, 90–91
Coffee liqueur
  Mudslide, 57
Cosmo, Raspberry, 55
Cranberry juice
  Raspberry Cosmo, 55
  Spiced Wassail, 86
Creamsicle, 35
Crème Brûlée, 40
Crème de menthe
  Grasshopper Pie, 43–44

E, F
Eggnog Rum, 82
Fourth of July, Berry, 79

G
Gelatin. *See also individual recipes*
  common mistakes with, 13–15
  refrigerating, 8, 9
  removing from molds, 11
  storing, 14
  unflavored, 8
Ginger ale
  Pomegranate Berry Salad, 18
  Sparkling Champagne and Strawberries, 49
Gingerbread Men, 84

Graham crackers
  Key Lime Pie, 33–34
  Peanut Butter and Jelly, 100–101
Grape-flavored gelatin
  Peanut Butter and Jelly, 100–101
Grapes
  White Sangria, 47
Grasshopper Pie, 43–44
Green Milk Tea, 31

H, I
Hot Chile Chocolate, 83
Ice cream
  Berry Fourth of July, 79
  Creamsicle, 35
  Green Milk Tea, 31
  Minty Watermelon Ice Cream, 68–69
  Root Beer Float Squares, 95–96
Irish cream liqueur
  Mudslide, 57

J, K
Jell-O. *See* Gelatin
Kahlúa, Coffee, 56
Key Lime Pie, 33–34

L
Ladyfingers
  Tiramisu, 90–91
Layers, creating, 12–13
Lemon Poppy Seed, 32
Limes
  Key Lime Pie, 33–34
  Mojito, 50
  Petite Watermelons, 89
Lychee and Pear Martini, 53

M

Mandarin oranges
    Creamsicle, 35
    Orange Chocolate, 66–67
Maple Soy Agar, 113
Marshmallow Butterscotch, 104
Martini, Pear and Lychee, 53
Million Dollar Gelatin, 21
Mimosa, 46
Mint
    Minty Watermelon Ice Cream, 68–69
    Mojito, 50
Mistakes, common, 13–15
Mojito, 50
Molds
    chilling, 12
    finding, 10
    layered, 12–13
    removing gelatin from, 11
    sizes of, 10, 12
Mudslide, 57

N

New York Cheesecake, 97
Nutella, Strawberry, 102–3
Nuts 'n' Honey, 25

O

Oats
    Nuts 'n' Honey, 25
Orange-flavored gelatin
    Orange Spice, 26
Oranges and orange juice
    Creamsicle, 35
    Mimosa, 46
    Orange Chocolate, 66–67
    Spiced Wassail, 86

P

Panna cotta
    Chai Tea Panna Cotta, 41
    Vanilla Clementine Panna Cotta, 114
Peaches
    Orange Spice, 26
    Peaches and Cream, 61–62
Peach schnapps
    Peaches and Cream, 61–62
Peanut butter
    Chocolate Peanut Butter Cups, 99
    Peanut Butter and Jelly, 100–101
Pear and Lychee Martini, 53
Pecans
    Carrot Cake, 23–24
    Maple Soy Agar, 113
    Million Dollar Gelatin, 21
    Nuts 'n' Honey, 25
Petite Watermelons, 89
Piña Colada, 52
Pineapple
    fresh vs. canned, 15
    Million Dollar Gelatin, 21
    Piña Colada, 52
    Watermelon Basil Agar, 111
Pomegranate Berry Salad, 18
Poppy Seed, Lemon, 32
Pumpkin Pie, 81

R

Rainbow Mold, Classic, 71–72
Raspberries
    Chocolate Raspberry Mousse Cups, 37–38
    Coconut Raspberry Agar, 107–8
    Raspberry Cosmo, 55
Rhubarb Rosemary Agar, 112
Root Beer Float Squares, 95–96

Rum
    Eggnog Rum, 82
    Mojito, 50
    Orange Spice, 26
    Piña Colada, 52
    Spiced Wassail, 86

S

Samoa, 92–93
Sangria, White, 47
Sparkling Champagne and Strawberries, 49
Spiced Wassail, 86
Strawberries
    Berry Fourth of July, 79
    Brains!!!, 80
    Petite Watermelons, 89
    Sparkling Champagne and Strawberries, 49
    Strawberry Nutella, 102–3
    White Sangria, 47
Strawberry-flavored gelatin
    Brains!!!, 80
    Petite Watermelons, 89

T

Tarts
    New York Cheesecake, 97
    Pumpkin Pie, 81
Tea
    Chai Tea Panna Cotta, 41
    Green Milk Tea, 31
Tiramisu, 90–91
Triple sec
    Raspberry Cosmo, 55

V

Vanilla Clementine Panna Cotta, 114
Vanilla wafers
    Banana Cream Pie, 73–75

Vegan recipes, 105
    Coconut Raspberry Agar, 107–8
    Maple Soy Agar, 113
    Rhubarb Rosemary Agar, 112
    Vanilla Clementine Panna Cotta, 114
    Watermelon Basil Agar, 111
Vodka
    Brains!!!, 80
    Mudslide, 57
    Pear and Lychee Martini, 53
    Petite Watermelons, 89
    Raspberry Cosmo, 55

W

Walnuts
    Carrot Cake, 23–24
    Maple Soy Agar, 113
Wassail, Spiced, 86
Watermelon
    Minty Watermelon Ice Cream, 68–69
    Petite Watermelons, 89
    Watermelon Basil Agar, 111
White Sangria, 47
Wine
    Mimosa, 46
    Sparkling Champagne and Strawberries, 49
    White Sangria, 47

Y

Yogurt
    Blueberry Yogurt, 63
    Lemon Poppy Seed, 32
    Vanilla Clementine Panna Cotta, 114

Ten Speed Press and the Ten Speed Press colophon are registered trademarks of Random House, Inc.

Some of the recipes in this work were originally published on Victoria Belanger's website, jellomoldmistress.com.

Library of Congress Cataloging-in-Publication Data

Belanger, Victoria.
  Hello, jell-o! : 50+ inventive recipes for gelatin treats and jiggly sweets / Victoria Belanger.
      p. cm.
  Includes index.
   Summary: "The Jello Mold Mistress shares the secrets to creating inspired, modern gelatin mold desserts,
with fresh fruits and flavors, new twists on trendy treats, and artistic presentations"—Provided by publisher.
  1. Cooking (Gelatin) 2. Cooking (Puddings) 3. Desserts. I. Title. II. Title: Hello, jello.
  TX814.5.G4B45 2012
  641.86'4—dc23
                        2011034560

ISBN 978-1-60774-111-4
eISBN 978-1-60774-112-1

Printed in China
Design by Betsy Stromberg
Food styling by Kim Kissling
Prop styling by Emma Star Jensen

10 9 8 7 6 5 4 3 2

First Edition